CRADLES IN Q CITY
Adoption | Orphan Care | Missions | Hope

Printed in the United States of America

Table of Contents

We dedicate this book to America World Adoption Association, Love Without Boundaries and all organizations and individuals who strive to share the gift of hope.

The book you are about to read
is a compilation of authentic life stories.
The facts are true, and the events are real.
These storytellers have dealt with crisis, tragedy, abuse
and neglect and have shared their most private moments,
mess-ups and hang-ups in order for others to learn and
grow from them. In order to protect the identities of those
involved in their pasts, the names and details of some
storytellers have been withheld or changed.

INTRODUCTION

Several times a year, in partnership with orphanages around the world, groups of Americans set out on trips through Storyteller Missions to learn and share the stories of children awaiting adoption.

These are the stories of some of those volunteers.

They came from very different places, emotionally and geographically. They came to one orphanage in Q City, China.

They came home changed forever.

RIPPLE EFFECT
The Story of Erin
Written by Holly DeHerrera

She was a back-row baby.

In a room full of children abandoned or left in the care of the orphanage, crib after crib lined the back row with kids who didn't thrive. They didn't seem to have any future other than remaining in the back row.

"Please hold her, Erin," Charlotte said. "She hasn't been held in a year and a half. Well, before I held her yesterday, she hadn't." Charlotte's pained eyes told me that this was a matter of life and death. And that maybe some things can't be undone.

Baby Hope, as we named her, lay still like a doll in her white knit sweater jumper.

"She'll cry, but she needs to be held. She's just not used to it, and she'll be scared."

I nodded and stepped toward the crib, reached in and lifted her out, her warm back against my fingertips. Although at age 2, she should have pulled in and wrapped her small legs around my middle, she only pressed back, rigid as petrified wood, screams cutting through the room humming with workers.

"Shh. It's okay, sweet girl."

Charlotte told me about the previous day, when she'd spent hours with Baby Hope, holding her but not looking at her — because holding and looking were too much for a child unaccustomed to receiving either — and how that finally brought quiet but not peace. The softening wouldn't come easily after being allowed to harden for so long. At 6 months, this baby had surgery to correct or improve her spina bifida — and ever since, she had been left alone to heal. Evidently, the staff acted under the mistaken notion that holding her would harm her. They regarded her as fragile, like blown glass. The entire year and a half after surgery, her only contact with caregivers was for feedings, soiled diapers and clothing changes.

I shifted on the floor mat, trying to keep her from crying again. I intentionally avoided her gaze. After what felt like hours, she stopped crying and arching away from me. She sat resigned, on my lap, the warm weight of her head and back finally relaxing against the crook of my arm. I pulled out a small square of silky fabric with crinkly material inside and allowed my gaze to turn toward her. I rubbed the cloth gently over her fuzzy scalp and sang "Jesus Loves Me." I felt certain the words were true as Baby Hope looked up at me with her black eyes, pulled up at the edges and fringed with fine black lashes.

I leaned my face an inch closer. "What's this noise?" The fabric crackled as I scrunched it so near her chest.

Baby Hope focused in on the swatch of color. Her eyes opened a fraction wider, and then she did something the nannies later said had never happened before.

She laughed.

RIPPLE EFFECT

❧❧❧

Comfort zones are funny things. They don't just keep things inside, safe and contained. They keep things out. When Charlotte first sent me a message on Facebook about a trip to an orphanage in China, the same place where her adopted daughter had come from, I decided that it wasn't for me. It was fine for Charlotte and people like her, who didn't have my responsibilities. My four children needed me. Besides, I hated flying.

I sent her a quick response: "It just isn't the right time for me to join."

Charlotte responded with, "Just pray about it."

I clicked the little "x" on the top right side of the screen, closing the conversation on the screen as my answer to the proposition.

At home, I talked about it to my husband, Ted. He had been my sweetheart since high school. Ted was a steady accountant, someone I could count on for clarity and wisdom.

"She asked me to fly across the ocean, but I home-school, Ted. And James is only 3." I ticked the reasons off on my checklist, liking the solidity of my case. Nobody expected someone in my situation to gallivant across the world. That was for single people, and maybe retired folks and people like Charlotte, who managed to do it all. Not me.

Ted didn't agree or disagree. He just let me speak. It did nothing to settle the churning in my chest.

Charlotte wouldn't get the picture. She pestered me more than once over the next few weeks. Irritated, I shoved my phone in my purse and slammed my car door. That helped a little. I buckled myself in the driver's seat. I assured myself that God understood my life and my obstacles.

I drove to an appointment two hours away. The two hours of quiet would normally be rare and beautiful, but that day they screamed at me.

I clicked my phone awake at a stoplight and dialed my sister's number. I needed distraction. Something about the orphans and the idea that I might do some good kept asking me to pay attention.

My sister didn't pick up. So I called my other sister. No luck there, either. I called Ted, but he didn't answer. During that drive, and the entire six hours of being away from home, my phone didn't ring once — even though I left messages for all three people.

I snapped on the radio, turning it up louder than usual. Images of Chinese babies floated in my peripheral vision, so I stared straight ahead. *Just get where you need to go.* My phone dinged, indicating that I had a message. At the next red light, I pulled up the message. Charlotte again.

I read her text quickly: "Look, you're going to come up with a million reasons why you can't do it, but God can deal with every detail. If he's saying go, go. Your children will see you listening to God and doing something you didn't want to do. Doing something hard."

I swallowed against the lump in my throat. The light turned green, and I threw my phone onto the passenger seat. The words of a song came through the radio: "What are you afraid of? Don't be afraid to step out."

Are you trying to tell me something, God? I wasn't one of those "God told me" kinds of people. I didn't have a direct hotline with a clear connection. But something told me that he was speaking and asking me to listen. All the way home, the radio station played one song after another about stepping out in faith, having courage, doing what you're called to do and trusting in God, knowing he will strengthen you and provide. Tears streamed down my face the rest of the way home. I felt like God was asking me to do this thing, but still my fears played like a movie reel. The plane careening into the ocean. My children needing me and me being unable to get to them. *What should I do?*

I pulled into our driveway later that day feeling like a dishrag that had been washed, spun, wrung out and then pressed by a giant iron. I walked toward the front door, my heart a giant balloon in my chest. Ted stepped out and offered a smile. His gentle presence calmed me.

"You okay?"

After looking at my face, he must have wondered what calamity had met me at the doctor's appointment.

I poured out my confusion to him. He hugged me against his chest, and I listened to the slow *thump, thump, thump* of his heart, and he only said, "Wow." I knew from experience the commentary would come later, once he'd had time to process all my words.

That week dragged on, punctuated by tears as I became increasingly convinced about what I needed to do.

One evening, Ted looked at me from where he sat in the living room.

"I was just reading about Jesus saying to the Pharisees," he said, "'How many more signs do you need?' I was thinking that maybe you've had a lot of signs of what you need to do." He reached his hand across to cover mine, limp on the armrest of the couch. "Erin, do you really feel you can say no now?"

I shook my head, unable to talk at first. The incessant tears were back again, like an irritating friend who wouldn't get the point that she wasn't invited.

"No, I think I'd be disobeying God."

Ted rubbed his fingertips over my knuckles and nodded.

Can't go back on it now. I got up, opened the laptop and, hands shaking, filled in the fields required to apply to go on the trip to China.

Name. *Not me. People like me don't go across the world to a communist country to hold orphans.*

Why do you feel called to go*? I just do, darn it. I didn't want to, but the feeling won't go away.*

I finished the application and closed the lid, then shuffled into the kitchen like a wooden doll. Unable to think or act like an adult, I just sat in the middle of the kitchen and sobbed. I knew I'd done the right thing, but the fear was tangible and had a life of its own. I wondered if the horrible feeling would go away. I had eight months to get ready for the trip, and spending that entire time paralyzed with fear sounded awful to me.

Lord, I need your help here.

When Ted and I told our kids about the trip, they all cheered and began writing cards for the children I'd meet. Somehow, their approval eased some of the worry — I felt like we were all in this together, and the importance made it worth my time.

The day I left, fear took over again as I drove away from my family. *What if the plane crashes and I die, and my kids think I chose this trip over them?* I prayed as if my life actually did depend on it, and peace swirled into the spaces I'd allowed panic to occupy. My anxiety slowly diminished, like fog burned off by the sun.

As the plane descended into China, I looked out my window. The scenery stole my breath. Lush green, broken by the beautiful Great Wall, zigzagged up into the mountains, as if it were just that easy to construct walls up sheer cliffs. The tan-gray of the stone made a path that climbed and climbed. *I'm here. God, only you could have brought me here, made me face my fears and then showed me the beauty of what comes when we only just listen and do what you've asked us to do.*

Tears of gratitude blurred the scene but did nothing to take away its impact. The green of the land broke through the white layer of clouds, helping me realize how much bigger the green is compared to the gray doubts, if we only just trust God's bigger plan.

We had to take another plane to get into the smaller

town where the orphanage was. On that flight, our team was scattered throughout the plane. I sat next to an older Chinese woman. We communicated as best we could through hand motions. I clicked on my phone, pulling up pictures of my family. Then she did the same, the deep crinkles around her eyes showing her pride. We talked in this way throughout the trip and, with just an hour left in the flight, she pulled out a piece of paper from the seat pocket and began writing something in beautiful Chinese script. I tucked the note into my bag, treasuring it even without knowing what it said.

The landscape swelled and cracked. Ravines cut through the lush land.

When the plane touched down, I had a strong feeling that this trip would change me forever.

കകക

We checked into our hotel. The next morning, we left in a vehicle that bumped toward the orphanage. As we arrived, I realized that the property included several tall buildings, all surrounded by a fence, which seemed to be wrapping the space in protective arms. A gate barred the entrance, where heartbroken parents often dropped off babies before first light.

The director told us about the children, and his love and concern for them were clear. We went inside, and my hands shook a little.

"This is where the new children are examined." The

dark-haired man ushered us into a small space. "These two were dropped off today."

I watched as the medical professional looked over one of the babies, peered into her ears and throat and held her miniscule foot between his thumb and middle finger. I looked around at our group and noticed my roommate wiping away tears. After the tour, we divided into our predetermined groups. I stood next to my roommate, needing the comfort of familiarity.

"Erin, I need to switch up the teams," Charlotte told me. "I'll need you in the baby room with this group." She pointed to several team members whom I didn't know well. My roommate wouldn't be part of my team after all.

I smiled. "Sure, wherever you need me to go."

We walked into the stark space lined with cribs, several babies in walkers on one side of the room. Looking at their sweet faces, dark eyes and fringes of black, fuzzy hair, I was struck by their beauty. Like the beautiful foggy green of the forest against the periwinkle sky I'd seen while we descended into this small province, the scene in that baby room stuck in my mind like a still photo that I suspected would never leave me. More than three-quarters of the little ones in the room had cleft palates, their small mouths pulled up in the middle. I realized that the cost of health care for babies such as these would likely prove too daunting for many parents, which probably explained their prevalence.

I spent the whole afternoon holding children, praying for each one, feeling a sense of purpose strong as a wall leading up a mountain, knowing that this place, so very far from my own babies, was just the place I needed to be. I felt that I was right where God's heartbeat could be heard. His love had drawn me there when my own will had told me not to go. *Thank you, Lord.*

That night, Charlotte called a meeting. "There is this little girl. We're calling her Baby Hope because she is part of a group of kids in the back row of the room who seemingly don't have much or any hope. The nannies are so busy with the children that they have to prioritize. They told me at first she couldn't be held, thinking she couldn't handle it, I suppose. That she had surgery. But when we started asking a few questions, it became apparent that she'd had surgery over a year and a half ago." Charlotte looked down at her hands and swallowed. She looked up again. "She needs to be held. She needs to be touched. It's been too long." She told us about how she spent hours holding the little girl only to be met with screaming. "So I just walked around the room and didn't look at her. We need to hold her as much as we can while we're here. Otherwise, I just don't think it will happen at all."

The next day, I held Baby Hope. At first, she screamed and hit herself in the head. Terror caused her to push against my chest like her life depended on it, but then she stopped fighting and her body relaxed. And then she laughed — the bubbling up kind of laughter that can't be helped. I crinkled the small square of material. She giggled like it was the funniest thing in the world. And maybe it was. Maybe the laughing came because someone had stopped to notice her, to look at her for more than just the minute it takes to change a diaper, allowing her to see that there was a world beyond the flat mattress she'd always known. My heart physically hurt looking down at the tiny coils of her ears, her paper-thin fingernails, her small body. She was so vulnerable, so precious, and a year and a half of having only her very basic needs met had taken its toll.

Members of our team continued to hold Baby Hope. As her world changed, so did mine. That next day, I went into the baby room and met little Jian. He stood on tiptoe in his walker, pressing his feet up and down, bouncing with his arms stretched out. I walked over to him. He looking up at me with a wide open-mouth smile, his lip cleft.

"Hi there, little one." I reached down and picked him up. He looked at me as if we were old friends, his dark eyes taking in my features. His thin black eyebrows rose up a fraction. "Hi," I whispered in awe. The connection didn't sizzle off like fog — it got stronger. I returned to Jian every day. It got to the point that when I set Jian down to give another child attention, he cried and lifted his arms as if to remind me that we'd made a commitment to one another.

"All right," I said. "I can hold two of you at the same time." And I hunkered down on the mat with two babies in my arms.

Jian spent all his time with me after that, telling me with his cries or his smiles that he wanted all of my attention. The other team members teased and called him my baby. I held Jian as he slept against my shoulder. He squeezed my finger and giggled. I rubbed my thumb over his velvety soft skin. As our time at the orphanage neared an end, it became harder and harder to leave Jian. The night before our departure, I sat on my bed and said to Charlotte, "How possible is it for me to adopt Jian?"

Before she even said anything, I saw the regret in the slight pinch above her eyes. "It's really unlikely, Erin. I mean, God can do anything. We've seen that. But picking out a specific child is actually not allowed. So getting him would be near impossible. Besides, the paperwork is very involved, and it would be at least a year before anything happened. It would take a miracle."

I buried my face in my hands and cried. I'd fallen in love with a child I could not choose, one I probably would never see again after going home. The ache pressed against my chest, and I sobbed harder. All through the night, long after Charlotte had left for her own room, I poured out my grief. *God, I feel like he belongs to me. Please help me to bear this. Help me to let him go.*

The next morning, I sat like a blob at the hotel breakfast area, the rest of the team talking between bites. I felt childish, exposed and raw. *What kind of person goes across the world and thinks she can just pick out a baby to take home like a souvenir?* I wondered. I hadn't expected the depth of connection I felt with Jian. The pain of loving that little boy, as short as our time had been together, seared something in me.

How can I love him so much, Lord? How can I stand

to say goodbye? I looked down at my plate and closed my eyes. I couldn't cry again. The skin under my eyes burned, and I tried to keep from touching it. I pulled out my phone and texted my husband: "Please pray. I'm having a really hard time today."

We rode in the van to the orphanage, and the city slipped by. Industrial-style buildings rubbed sides with ornate plush gardens. Gold and red-orange structures with tops like a queen's crown reached up to the sky. Behind the bustle of Q City stood the orange, rocky hillsides tangled with green. I twisted my wedding ring, praying and praying. *Help me, Jesus. I can't do this without your help.*

Charlotte looked over at me and said, "Today you can pick whichever room you'd like. Take some time to say goodbye." She then returned her gaze to the front.

I nodded, confirming in my mind that letting go made the most sense. Holding on, even a little bit, would only shred me from the inside out. And Ted didn't even know what I'd been feeling. I needed to talk to him in person. He might not even want to adopt. I swallowed against a new swell of tears.

Our group split off to different rooms. I knew where I needed to go. I needed to say goodbye. Jian saw me and reached up from his place in his walker. I hooked my hands under his arms and gently tugged him to my chest, nuzzling his soft cheek with mine. I spent the day walking with him, talking to him, praying for him and for whoever would have him as part of their family someday. I prayed that they'd love him and teach him about Jesus, that they'd tell him that his life had purpose and value, and that God saw him and heard his cries. Peace began to filter in like tiny fans of light around the edges of a dark silhouette.

I rubbed his small head with my free hand, and I sang, "I will give you peace, when the walls come crashing down …" The words were for me as much as for Jian. I felt the gentle hands of God touching the ache in my chest and replacing it with calm and understanding. I pressed a kiss to Jian's temple and set him down.

"Goodbye, sweet boy. I love you."

I relied on God's strength to help me walk out. I reminded myself to trust that the one who'd called me to go to China in the first place would take care of this little boy. I have no doubt that God saw these children and knew their futures. He only asked me to step in and do my part by showing them love.

As our plane pulled up into the clouds, I pulled out my journal. I wrote about my experience in China and the people I'd met, and I wrote about Jian and about letting him go. I turned my face to the green still visible below and whispered, "I'll be back, China." Something had begun in me, like the falling of dominoes. I knew my life would never go back to what it had been. The neat, orderly picture had been shattered, and I realized that God was building something brand-new.

Back home, I hugged my own babies, letting their warmth seep into my chest. I hugged my husband and told him about my experiences, but I only said, "I have a heart for adoption." I didn't tell him right away that my heart had been practically torn in half meeting a little boy who somehow seemed to belong to me. But over time, I shared more details until the whole truth was out.

Ted said he'd pray about it, and he did. He prayed for two long months. During that time, I was told that someone else whose adoption paperwork was already complete had shown interest in little Jian. I prayed and trusted that God had a special destiny for that boy and that I could rely on him to work all things out for the best.

Bible verses that I'd never really latched on to or paid much attention to before started popping out at me. James 1 reads, "Take care of the widows and orphans." *God's heart for his people needed to be mine.* I wanted what was important to him to be important to me. I wanted his mission to become my own. Time crawled on like cold honey pouring from a jar. I knew the sweetness would come, but waiting filled me with impatience.

The new year began. Ted took my hand and said, "I've been praying, and I feel like we have all these blessings. We need to share them. The Bible says, 'Do not neglect to do good and to share what you have, for such sacrifices are pleasing to God.' So I think we need to adopt."

I felt like the floor had dropped out from under me, but the invisible hand of God held me up. "You mean, down the road?"

He smiled and shook his head. "Like, now."

I screamed and wrapped my arms around his neck. "Thank you!" Tears made the words difficult.

That night, I began the lengthy paperwork process. I submitted the application the next day, and we were approved to begin. I picked up the phone and reached the woman in charge of our application.

"Is there any way we can be matched with Jian?" I asked.

She hesitated and said, "It has to be initiated by the orphanage. We can't ask for him. And there are several families ahead of you for a boy that age."

I hung up and reminded myself once again to trust God to do what was best for us and for Jian, whatever that might be.

The next morning, we told the kids. "Daddy and I have decided that God wants us to adopt a baby from China."

Cheers erupted around the breakfast table.

"You know the little boy I told you about? I feel we are supposed to adopt him," I said. "But that might not happen. Let's just pray for God to work out everything the way he wants, okay?"

My little James prayed then. "I pway baby Jian Lee will get to come to our house."

The rest of the kids nodded and grinned. No doubt or hesitation.

James prayed that same prayer every night before bed and at every meal following the announcement.

I called Charlotte in the midst of more paperwork and documentation. "I'm overwhelmed by all this. How long will it take? I feel like the more time that goes by, the less likely it is that we'll get Jian."

"Hmm. Well, it usually takes six months to just get your packet to China, Erin. But remember, if God wants you to be matched with him, he'll work all that out."

In February, we received the news that Baby Hope had passed away. Her story had reached many hearts — several people were even looking into the possibility of adopting her. My heart broke when I heard the news. *Why, God? Why, when she could have experienced a life of love after so much neglect?* But even in praying, I sensed the answer. Baby Hope's story had been shared with thousands and had stirred many people to consider adoption, bringing new hope to a whole orphanage of children. I believe her life purpose had been for hope and that her homecoming to God had been a joyful one. No more lying in the back row — she had gone home to Jesus.

Two and a half months later, our paperwork was sent over to China. It happened in less than half the time it was supposed to — but I knew that, with others in front of us and the adoption agency pairing up completed files with those children listed as ready to be adopted, the likelihood of Jian being matched with us was slight.

Ted and I had a cruise planned. I figured I could rest while we floated off into the ocean, knowing that I'd done all I could on my end and that our complete paperwork had been sent to the right people. All we could do was wait. The dossier had been mailed to China on April 30, and we left for our cruise May 1.

Ted and I entered our cabin after a day in the sunshine, and I sat down with the laptop. Something compelled me to open my email, despite the zero percent chance of having any news.

But the email popped up: "Your dossier has been logged in. You're now eligible to be matched."

I looked over at Ted and pointed. He rubbed my shoulders and planted a kiss on my cheek. I tried to prepare myself for a match with another child. God had a purpose and a plan for every one of the kids in the orphanage. I didn't want to be willing and waiting only for Jian. Maybe God had different plans. I wanted to be ready and excited no matter what child they matched with us.

So far, Jian's file hadn't been listed, meaning he couldn't be matched with anyone. But even if his file was listed, the adoptions went in the order they were received, and I knew we weren't first in line. I rubbed my hands on my shorts and then snapped my laptop shut, determined to leave the outcome in God's hands.

Later that day, like a woman deranged, I clicked into my email account again. Another email popped up in bold black letters. It was from the adoption agency.

"Jian Lee's file has come in, and he is now eligible to be matched with your family."

Again, I turned to my husband. This time, I screamed. I stood and hugged him and cried. God had pushed me out of my comfort zone, asked me to trust him, opened my heart to what his heart loved and allowed me to fall in love with a little boy in China. And now that little boy would be ours! I later learned that there were only three families, including us, with login dates waiting to be matched with boys, and only three boys' files came in that day. The two families before us had been matched with two other boys even though Jian had been listed at the same time. That's what allowed us, impossibly so, to be matched with the one child who already belonged to my heart.

In August, Ted, my middle daughter and I boarded a plane to go get our child. The plane lifted us into the clouds, and we soared back to China and to the city I fell in love with less than a year earlier. When they brought Jian to us, I reached out for him, grateful for the gift I had received.

In trusting God, I allowed myself to see how deeply he loves his children.

I saw his amazing provision.

I saw that living in my own neat world wasn't good enough — not for me or for my kids.

I learned through the resisting and then stepping out, the retreating and opening of closed hands, the sobbing in a kitchen and the lifting of my head to see the beauty of a dense, green mountainside. I learned from looking only at my own children's faces to looking at faces that were very different — most considered by the world to be less than perfect — including a little girl named Hope. I learned the height, depth and breadth of God's amazing love.

And I learned to never, ever underestimate the ripple effect of trusting God.

CLARITY AND STRENGTH
The Story of Brian
Written by Adam Knechtel

My hands shook violently, and I felt sweat pouring down my face. I couldn't avoid it any longer. This was it — the moment to ask.

"So, uh, there's actually a reason I asked you to lunch today," I started. "I think you're great — in fact, I've thought so for a long time. But, as I've gotten to know you better over these last few years, and especially as I've gotten to know you better on these medical mission trips, I've become even more impressed with everything about you — your heart for children, your willingness to serve, your kindness, gentleness and grace — and I was just wondering, I mean, I was curious … well, I just wanted to ask — would you like to date me?"

Alyssa leaned back in her chair, appearing somewhat startled. Then she flashed a sweet smile as her cheeks turned the slightest shade of red.

"I have to be honest," she replied. "When you said you wanted to talk about some things from the trip, I thought you meant logistically." She laughed. "I thought you wanted to talk about some of the stuff we learned along the way. I had no idea *this* is what you meant!"

❧ ❧ ❧

Alyssa and I met in med school. She studied pediatrics, and I was in family medicine.

The medical department had a strong connection with the Christian Medical and Dental Association and offered a variety of mission trips to medical students each year during the campus-wide spring break. Alyssa and I, both heavily involved with our local churches and various organizations on campus, were thrilled to learn about the opportunity. We both immediately committed, and when March rolled around, Alyssa and I joined roughly 40 other medical or dental students and 10 practicing doctors and dentists. We packed our bags, loaded onto a plane and headed to South America.

That first trip was unlike anything I'd ever experienced in my life. Almost as soon as we checked into our hotel, we split off into smaller groups of four or five students per every couple of practicing physicians. Then we headed off into the city and surrounding tribal areas to administer basic medical and dental aid to all who needed it. Hour after hour, day after day, we treated anyone and everyone who came forward. Many were children. None could have afforded even the most basic care we offered on their own.

I saw the amazement in their eyes as they stared into mine. I felt the depth of gratitude when they hugged me or shook my hand. I sensed the joy in their hearts as they left our clinics in less pain or discomfort and with medicine to treat their ailments and illnesses.

At the same time, I felt my own heart break for these people. If only they had access to basic medical treatment, most of their suffering could have been alleviated much sooner. Fractured bones that were never properly set couldn't fully heal. Minor cuts and scrapes became infected and spread disease due to a lack of proper cleaning. Teeth rotted and fell out due to a lack of toothpaste and toothbrushes.

They suffered, even the children, day in and day out under conditions that should have been easily and inexpensively avoidable.

God, I prayed. *Why do these little ones live through such turmoil when I was born and raised in a much more comfortable situation?*

I couldn't answer the question on my own, so I fell back on a truth I had clung to for many years.

Lord, I don't know the answer to that question. And although I want to think deeply about these things, I know that I must live simply in obedience to you. You are good. You are loving. You are in control. You have a plan, both for me and for these people. Please give me abundant clarity to trust in you, to follow you and to live for you.

We continued to serve these people until the week ended and we left for home. I boarded that return flight a forever-changed man.

కొ·కొ·కొ

The following year, again in March, Alyssa and I traveled with the CMDA to administer medical aid to a hurting community. About halfway through the weeklong trip, we found ourselves with a day off. It was a time to relax, prepare, rest or study as we saw fit. I walked from room to room in the hotel, asking my colleagues about their plans for the day. I finally stumbled upon Alyssa in the lobby and asked her about her plans.

"Well," she began, "I know a few people are just relaxing in their rooms for the day. Some are down by the pool. And I think a small group is heading into town to do some shopping."

"What about you?" I inquired.

"Well, actually, I'm going to visit a local orphanage and spend some time with the kids. You're welcome to join me if you'd like!"

I'd wanted to spend more time with Alyssa, but most of the time, we were so busy that I could only manage brief meetings in between our heavy workloads.

"I'd love to," I shot back. "When are you leaving?"

"I'm just waiting for the cab now. If you need to go change or grab anything, you've probably got a few minutes. Meet back here in five?"

I nodded and set off toward my room.

&ponponpon;

As the cab slowed to a stop, I bent forward slightly until I could see the orphanage through the dust-covered window. It was a massive structure, almost like a school, with a large grassy hill on one side and a well-manicured lawn on the other. An impressive playground sat in the middle of the campus, and an array of plants lined the outer fence and driveway.

Inside, small cubbies lined the hallways. Each cubby was filled with backpacks, shoes and various other personal items. Art projects hung on the walls. We passed several rooms, each filled with assorted toys and learning materials suitable for various age groups. We saw several women working there and introduced ourselves.

A Catholic organization ran the orphanage, and Alyssa and I immediately felt the love of Christ there. These women clearly loved each child as their own and provided for them as best they could. Each child was fed and clothed and kept warm and healthy.

Unfortunately, there were simply too many children and too few staff. The women who worked there could not possibly devote the personal attention that each child required and desired. I wondered whether the children had anyone to ask how their day was going, or if they had learned anything new, or what they were dealing with, or what they feared. Their hunger for attention was almost palpable.

Alyssa immediately walked over to a group of kids, sat down and began playing with them. She talked to them, laughed with them, chased them around and drew out the shy ones. As I watched her, I thought, *That's what absolute, unconditional love looks like.*

I knew that she had a heart for orphans and children in general. We both grew up in Christian households and were familiar with passages in the Bible emphasizing the importance of caring for the fatherless and the orphaned and the downtrodden. We'd had several conversations about these things. I'd seen her heart break for the suffering children a year before on our first mission trip. At the orphanage, once again, I saw that same unyielding affection blossom in front of these children.

The same questions that had sprung up a year before once again arose in my mind.

Lord, why was I blessed to be born into such an incredible, loving family? Why weren't these kids blessed in the same measure? Why couldn't they have been given the same sort of love and comfort?

As before, my prayer shifted.

I can't answer these questions, Lord, but you can. You are good to these children just as you are good to me. You love these children the same as you love me. You are in control of their lives just as you are mine. As sure as you have a plan for me, you have a plan for them. Please, give me abundant clarity to see that and believe it. And please give me the strength to do something about it.

ৡৡৡ

Alyssa and I began dating shortly after returning home from that second trip. We continued to progress through our studies, and each March, we'd join with the CDMA to spend a week ministering medically and spiritually to broken and suffering people across South America.

We married just months before our fourth and final

trip during our last year of med school, and we got to spend the entire week together.

Our group that year focused on reaching farther into the jungle than we had ventured before. The plan was to meet up with a group of missionaries who would take us to meet a local tribe. We loaded ourselves and our gear into several narrow boats, each outfitted with a small motor on the back, and slowly made our way down the Amazon River through a network of tributaries. Along the way, we encountered freshwater dolphins and various other jungle inhabitants. Finally, we came across a small village built just off the banks of the river.

We spent the entire day providing medical assistance to as many people as we could serve. At night, we set up our camp inside their small, recently erected church building. It was nothing more than a simple wooden room raised up on stilts so as not to be destroyed by the river when it overflowed its banks.

As we laid down for the night, spraying ourselves with insect repellant and wrapping ourselves securely in our mosquito nets, Alyssa and I talked to each other about the day's events.

We talked about the mosquitoes and how much of a public health menace they were. We talked about the people we had treated. We talked about the various aches and pains we felt after working long hours. We talked, once again, about the plight of the children in these tribes and communities.

"Brian," she began, after a brief moment of silence.

"I've been thinking about something, and I wanted to share it with you."

I nodded for her to continue.

"Ever since we visited that orphanage in our second year, I've felt a deep longing in my heart to help out in some way. I know that we participate in these trips every year, and that's great, but I want to do something a little longer lasting, a little more intentional. I know we can't yet adopt children for ourselves, as we're still in the middle of our medical training, but we can at least get involved financially somehow — and maybe, down the road, we can look into adopting for ourselves. What do you think?"

"Alyssa, I've felt the exact same way!"

Visiting that orphanage had challenged me deeply.

I always knew that God cared for orphans and wanted us to do the same, but when I actually saw those children, spent time with them and felt their sorrow, it became a real, tangible understanding rather than some abstract, philosophical concept.

"We absolutely need to get involved any way we can."

She smiled, quietly rolled closer to me and wrapped me in her arms. I gave her a soft kiss on the forehead.

"But as for now," I continued, "with the heat and the humidity and the mosquitoes, I don't think we'll ever get to sleep."

"Me, either," she replied. "I'm terribly exhausted from today, but I'm not sure I'll be comfortable enough to rest."

Yet within seconds, we both closed our eyes and drifted off to sleep.

CLARITY AND STRENGTH

❧❧❧

Over the next several years, we researched various orphanages and agencies and committed financial support as we finished medical school in Oklahoma, moved to San Antonio to start and finish our residencies, and then packed up for Louisiana. Alyssa had joined the Army, which provided her with a scholarship for med school, and this was her first active-duty assignment.

In the coolness of early April, before the southern heat and humidity had set in for the summer, we found out that Alyssa was pregnant with twins. The months rolled by, and everything progressed beautifully. On the day before Thanksgiving, we welcomed our daughters, Gracie and Lucy, into the world.

Alyssa's parents and sister drove down on Thanksgiving Day, stopping by Cracker Barrel on their way to pick up a holiday feast, which they brought to the hospital. Shortly thereafter, my parents and brother joined us. As my mother entered our room and saw the girls for the first time, she lost her breath and stood perfectly still for a brief moment. With tears of joy welling up in her eyes, she stared down at them and exclaimed, "My goodness, they are absolutely, perfectly beautiful!" Alyssa agreed. I agreed. And my mother rushed in to hold her precious grandchildren.

Around the same time that Alyssa got pregnant, her sister and brother-in-law decided to adopt a child from Haiti. As we progressed through our pregnancy, they progressed through the adoption process. They inspired us, and we bombarded them with questions. In every moment, they were eager to share with us what they were learning, even when they encountered struggles or setbacks.

"You're going to get to a place where you feel frustrated," they explained. "Your paperwork has been turned in for so long, for example, but no progress has been made and no updates have been given. You'll want answers and will have nowhere to turn. It will happen. Just take a step back, breathe and trust in God. He's helped you begin this journey, and he will see it through to the end. Just keep going."

They continued to offer such guidance and support. "Here's what we went through …" or, "Here's what you can expect when …" or, "Here's some things that frustrated us." As they labored through the ups and downs of the adoption process, they shared their journey with us.

Within a month after our girls were born, they were able to pick up their son, Robbie, in Haiti. That Christmas, our entire family got to meet him for the first time, and our hearts were completely enraptured by the incredible little life before us.

The Army transferred Alyssa back to our home state of Oklahoma. Our girls came to know and love Robbie, just as we did. Alyssa and I remained interested in someday adopting a child, and we continued to ask Robbie's parents questions at every turn.

"Don't be afraid to ask for help," Alyssa's sister

encouraged us one day. "We've been so blessed to have a huge support group behind us. Our church, our family and all our friends came forward in a big way to help. We were hesitant to ask at first, but we quickly found out that people are aching to help — they just don't know how. People were willing to mow our yard, bring us meals or clean up our house ... just to help smooth out the transition in any way possible. And all of it, every little gesture and sacrifice, went a long way!"

Encouraged, Alyssa and I prayed about our next steps. "Father, we've read the Bible, and we've seen your heart for the fatherless. You've introduced us to orphaned children and have broken our hearts toward them. You've blessed us to see someone walk the path before us. You've given us the knowledge, the compassion, the desire and the guidance to pursue this in our own life — and we want to move forward. We want to open our home to these children, to open our hearts, our lives and our family to them. Please help us do this. Give us abundant clarity as we move forward. Give us wisdom to remember the advice we've been given. Give us patience and faith as we encounter frustrations. Give us strength as we grow weak and weary. Amen."

☙☙☙

"Hey, honey! You're looking beautiful today!" I exclaimed. Alyssa's miniature face lit up with a smile on the computer screen.

"Why, thank you!" she said, laughing.

"Hi, Mommy!" Gracie and Lucy yelled in unison while climbing over each other on my lap, trying to get a closer view of the screen.

"There are my beautiful girls! Hi, Gracie! Hi, Lucy! Have you both been good for Daddy today?"

They both nodded their heads and looked to me for confirmation.

"They've been wonderful." I smiled. "How's your day been?"

"Hot, as usual," she answered. "But it's been great! God has granted me safety, security and the ability to help others, so I can't complain."

Alyssa was about halfway through a seven-month deployment to Afghanistan. The girls had taken it pretty well, being old enough to understand that she was doing important work helping our soldiers, but not quite old enough to understand that she was in any danger. By God's grace, she was stationed in an urban center and had access to a computer and Internet, so we often spent our evenings video-calling each other.

The girls and I set up our laptop at the kitchen table to "have dinner" with Mommy.

Afterward, we all played hide-and-seek. The girls ran off into a different room. A few seconds later, I followed with the computer held out in front of me.

"Are they behind the couch?" Alyssa asked as I peeked behind the sofa.

"No."

The girls squealed and giggled.

"Are they behind the counter?"

"No." Another round of cackles.

"Are they under the table?" Alyssa finally questioned as I popped down beneath the table to find a pair of sheepish faces turning and hiding, then bursting out in laughter.

Later that night, we put them to bed with one of their favorite stories. Alyssa had memorized a handful of them, so I balanced the laptop on my knees, held a book in front of the girls and turned the pages as Alyssa recited the story in full.

We spent nearly every night in similar fashion, and our family routine didn't suffer despite Alyssa being gone for nearly six months.

Neither did our adoption process. Shortly before her deployment began, Alyssa and I had researched various adoption agencies. We settled on America World Adoption Association, and we began filling out the application. As the months ticked by, we processed countless forms and inquiries after putting the girls to bed.

We knew about the possible frustrations we'd encounter, so we never felt blindsided by any setback or delay. Having been encouraged to continue ceaselessly in prayer, we relied wholly on God — not ourselves or our knowledge or our agency — for clarity and wisdom and patience.

By late autumn, as we video-called one evening, we opened an email from AWAA that stated we had finally been matched up with a son, Taylor, and a daughter, Naomi, both of whom lived in China. We were ecstatic to finally reach this point — to be blessed with two new beautiful children waiting for us halfway across the world after years of growing desire and eager prayerfulness. I jumped around the house, hooting and hollering, while Alyssa cheered triumphantly on the screen. After our initial emotional eruption, I read aloud the final line of the message informing us that, due to processing time frames for two-child adoptions and our family's stage in that process, travel would not likely be until October of the following year.

"October of next year?" I repeated. "That's nearly an entire year away! Why can't we just get them now?"

Alyssa sank back into her chair.

"My sister warned me about this," she started. "She said even once you're matched up, the process can take a while. Just like a biological pregnancy takes nine months, an adoption — or paper pregnancy, as they call it — takes time. We'll get through this, though, just like every hurdle before."

Her faithful resolve encouraged me. We prayed once more for clarity and strength, thanked the Lord for having answered our prayers and said goodbye. I powered off the laptop and headed to bed, longing for October.

෨෨෨

I sat impatiently, drumming my right foot against the carpet while patting my hands against my thighs.

"You know," Alyssa said, leaning over, "nervously turning yourself into a human instrument isn't going to make her get here any faster." She winked.

I couldn't help it. After months and months of waiting, October had finally arrived. In the previous 48 hours, Alyssa and I had boarded a plane for China, landed, gotten picked up by a translator at the airport, traveled to our nearby hotel, spent one sleepless night in restless anticipation, woke up early that morning and flew out to Naomi's province to pick her up.

Her orphanage was several hours away by car, so we passed the time in the fifth-floor seating area of our hotel with two other couples, all of us anxiously awaiting the arrival of our children. Our excitement increased as the minutes ticked by, until finally, the elevator doors opened and out stepped an orphanage worker cradling the most beautiful, precious little girl in her arms.

Alyssa and I stared at each other for a brief second before rushing over to meet the newest member of our family. The nanny gently placed Naomi in Alyssa's arms, congratulated us and stepped aside.

I stared down at Naomi and felt overcome with love.

Twenty months old and slowly overcoming a developmental delay, she was all of 15 pounds and looked incredibly fragile yet incredibly capable. A small cleft lip only made her more adorable than we could have ever imagined. The nanny taught us how to feed her using a special nursing bottle and explained through a translator that Naomi was not yet able to sit up or roll over. We thanked her, took Naomi back to our room and fell more in love by the minute. We soon discovered that she would only sleep for a couple hours at a time and much preferred to be held, walked or bounced while she was awake. Alyssa and I took turns walking her up and down the hotel hallways for an hour at a time while the other one slept. As the hours turned into days and the days turned into a week, we bonded more deeply. We learned her likes, her dislikes, her favorite way to be held, her feeding times — everything about her.

Eventually, the day came for us to fly to Taylor's province to pick him up. Before we left the hotel, we knelt down together with Naomi in our arms and prayed.

"Lord, thank you so much for blessing us with Naomi. Already, she brings so much happiness to our lives. We don't understand why her parents were not able to keep her, but we thank you that you watched over her and brought her to us. We thank you that her parents cared enough to place her into someone's care. We thank you that they did the best they could to provide a future and hope for her. We believe that Naomi is a gift to us, just as Gracie and Lucy are. Thank you for giving us the privilege to raise this little girl as our own, to care for her, watch over her and protect her as you do us. Please give us the strength and the ability to do so. Thank you for this wonderful, miraculous blessing. Amen."

Later that day, we arrived at a second hotel where we

would meet our son, Taylor. The same nervous anticipation gripped us until the elevator finally opened once more and in walked a stout, strong little boy wearing a bright yellow jacket and a Mickey Mouse backpack.

"There he is!" I shouted with joy. "There's Taylor!"

Led by his nanny, Taylor came right up to us and shyly looked us over.

We offered him an assortment of small toys and snacks. Before long, he seemed completely comfortable in our presence.

The next few days were both a challenge and a blessing. Taylor, who was six months older than Naomi, instantly became attached to her and looked after her like an older brother, even offering her some of his snacks if he had extra. However, Naomi's sleeping issues continued, so Alyssa and I requested two adjoining rooms, allowing one of us to sleep through the night with Taylor while the other comforted Naomi. Just as when we ministered to the children in those South American villages, and just as when we visited the orphans in that Catholic orphanage, and just as when we raised Gracie and Lucy, I noticed Alyssa's tremendous heart for children and was amazed and encouraged beyond belief. Although we struggled through sleepless nights and exhausting new challenges, our marriage only grew stronger as we worked together to care for the little ones entrusted to us. Each night, we would pray that same prayer over both children, thanking God for the blessing of calling them our own and pleading with him to lead us through this new stage of life.

After being alone with Naomi and Taylor for some time, we Skyped with our extended family back home and rejoiced as they expressed the same love and excitement as they did when Gracie and Lucy were born.

Before we left to come back home, Alyssa was able to visit Taylor's orphanage with him since it was just down the road.

"You would be amazed," she told me after returning for the day. "The level of care they show to these kids is incredible. They truly love every kid in there, and they were so excited to see Taylor again. They nicknamed him 'Old Ox' because of how strong he is. I saw his room, his bed, his nannies — everything!"

We made our way to the airport, grinning from ear to ear, recognizing that our journey was nearly complete. By God's grace and provision, we had finally come to adopt two precious children as our own. I fastened my seatbelt, glanced at Taylor, Naomi and Alyssa, and felt absolutely overjoyed.

❧❧❧

Nearly two years passed, and our family was happier and fuller than ever. Gracie and Lucy were thrilled to be older sisters and took to Naomi and Taylor instantly. They ran around the yard and through the house with Taylor as much as possible and laid down to cuddle and play with Naomi just as often. All four of them got along, and all four of them fought. All four of them shared, and all four of them were selfish. All of it warmed our hearts, for we knew that they truly considered each one to be their brother or sister just the same.

Even though we were delighted with the family that God had given us, we knew there were more children out there who needed a home — and we decided we had a home that needed more children. So, in the early stages of 2014, we brought home our fifth child, Luke, from the same orphanage that had given us Naomi. All four other children — acting like seasoned adoption veterans by this point — lovingly and excitedly welcomed him with open arms and joy-filled hearts. Luke, for his part, fell in love with them just as quickly.

Our family, regardless of shape, size, color or ability, grew closer together with each passing day. Alyssa and I quickly learned that everything that had seemed big and scary before we began this journey wasn't so big or scary after all. We relied on God to give us the strength, wisdom and clarity we needed every day. Many people approached us at church, at work or during family gatherings to tell us how much of a blessing we must be for these children and what a wonderful work we were doing. Every time, Alyssa and I chuckled to ourselves and set the record straight.

"No, no, no," we would answer. "Our kids bless us a hundred times more than we bless them. We get so much more out of these relationships and these blessings than they could ever hope to get from us. You've got it all backward." And it was true, all of it. God showed us his mercy, grace, love, kindness and provision every single day through our children — a blessing we could only hope to mimic in humble fashion with our roles as parents.

After putting the kids to sleep one night, we laid down in bed, and Alyssa placed her head on my chest.

"Sometimes I wish I could go back again," I started.

I felt her head turn slightly so she could look at me as I continued.

"It's just — we've only got a handful of pictures from Naomi and Taylor and Luke's first few years of life, before we adopted them, and … I just wish we had more. I wish I knew more about them when they were young. I wish I could have seen where they were from and what they liked to do and what made them feel happy and fulfilled and loved. Like you, when you got to visit Taylor's orphanage and talk to the women who raised him early on. I wish I had that."

"Then pray about it." She smiled. Then she sat up, placed her hand on my shoulder and gave me a goodnight kiss on the cheek. "But for now, let's get some sleep."

And with that, she rolled over and turned off the light.

৵৵৵

In October of the following year, I believe God answered that prayer. A division of AWAA called Storyteller Missions had been sending groups of people from all over the United States to visit orphanages across the world in the hopes that they could collect photos, videos and personal experiences of the children still needing to be matched with adoptive parents.

Their vision was that the potential adoptive parents, who might otherwise be worried or confused, might be encouraged and enlightened to hear stories of the children waiting to meet them. They could see pictures and videos of the children enjoying their favorite foods, playing with their favorite toys or overcoming their physical or mental hardships. Their vision, quite simply, was to encourage those back home as they awaited the twists and turns of international adoption — and I was more than thrilled when I got the opportunity to be a part of it.

While Alyssa volunteered with Love Without Boundaries, an organization that exists to provide nutritional, medical and educational support to orphaned and impoverished children throughout China, I found myself traveling to China with AWAA, visiting an orphanage in Q City to compile reports to send home to potential parents back in America.

Even more exciting was the fact that both Naomi and Luke had spent the first year of their lives in the Q City orphanage.

I stepped inside the orphanage, and my heart almost burst with joy. I paused and took it all in. *This is where they grew up. This is where they grew as happy 1-year-olds, learning and growing and being tenderly cared for and protected. Thank you, Lord! Thank you!*

The team and I spent the week doing medical assessments on the children — learning about them and loving on them.

"Despite her cleft lip and initial nutritional struggles,

she's growing up big and strong," I scribbled on a note card. An image of a beautiful little girl with sticky cheeks and fingers, a plate of dragon fruit sitting next to her on the table, accompanied my words. "She loves dragon fruit. It's her favorite food, and she just can't get enough!"

Next, I met a happy young boy who seemed to never tire. After recording a video of him running around the room and laughing heartily during a game of hide-and-seek, I jotted a quick line about how active he was. "He loves to run, jump and explore, never growing tired, never letting his development disorder slow him down."

"She's recognizing colors, shapes, words and numbers," I wrote underneath the image of a little girl holding up a pair of drawings she'd made earlier that day. "Not a day goes by that she fails to learn something new. Upon each discovery, her face lights up."

We met the most wonderful, adorable children, each with a unique story and struggle, each growing through and overcoming individual trials and circumstances. Day after day, I compiled notes, photographs and videos to send back home to hopeful future parents, who might be wrestling with doubt or uncertainty about the path they were traveling. I hoped to assuage their anxieties and offer a glimpse into the life of the delightful child they might soon adopt.

Before the trip was over, I asked our translator to help me speak to one of the nannies about my children.

I pulled up pictures of them on my phone. "I'm Naomi and Luke's father. Do you remember them?"

Our translator, Violet, rattled off my question, and the nanny smiled.

"She remembers!" Violet said. "Did you want to see their old cribs? They're just over here."

I couldn't help but smile as I opened the camera app on my phone and followed them both down the hall.

The nanny pointed to a small wooden toy on the dresser.

"This," Violet translated as the nanny spoke, "was his absolute favorite. He hardly ever put it down."

I picked up the small toy and looked it over in my hands. Then I took out my phone and snapped a picture. Already, I had a growing collection of photographs. I quickly flipped through the album on my phone, and a smile spread across my face.

"Was there anything else you wanted to see?" Violet asked, after a few moments of silence.

"Actually, I'd like to record a short video of all the nannies who remember my kids, if you wouldn't mind. You know, just to hear their stories about what they were like, what they enjoyed doing, what they loved about them — that sort of stuff."

"Absolutely!" Violet smiled. "Let's go grab a seat."

She motioned for me to follow and then made her way to the door. I took one last glance at the image of Luke's favorite wooden toy and smiled once again.

RELENTLESS LOVE
The Story of Katherine
Written by Arlene Showalter

"I lift up my eyes to the mountains — where does my
help come from? My help comes from the Lord,
the maker of heaven and earth."

I peered through the tiny airplane window at the
rugged mountains below. Jagged rocks split with deep
crevasses pushed toward the sky with a show of fixed
strength. My hands trembled as my favorite Psalm, 121,
came to mind.

*God made these awful, majestic, intimidating
mountains, mountains that tower over our destination.
How badly do I need his help now.*

"Almost there." Mark covered my hands with his
warm one. "Relax, Katherine."

"I wish I could."

"This is what we've waited and prayed for all these
years. And now the time is here." He squeezed my hand.
"Remember, God wouldn't bring us this far and not help
us. Would he?"

"No. No, he wouldn't."

We braced for landing and waited until the seatbelt
signs blinked off.

"Here we are." Mark grinned. "Let's go."

Yes. Here we are. In China with our two daughters to meet our new son.

I took a deep breath and released it in a long, measured exhale. *This is it.*

ॐॐॐ

"I wish I'd adopted a sister for you," my dad told me when I was 14 and an only child. "A little girl from China."

His words stayed in my heart. Years later, I shared them with Mark, my soldier fiancé.

"I think that's a cool idea," Mark responded.

"You'd be interested in adopting a baby girl from China?"

"Sure. My best friend growing up was from Taiwan, and I spent a lot of time in his home. I like the Asian culture. I think a Chinese baby would be perfect. But it would probably be best to put that dream on hold as long as I'm on active duty."

We married. We moved a lot. Our family grew as I gave birth to three children. And we continued to save money toward a future adoption.

ॐॐॐ

"The time is right," Mark announced after he moved from active duty to the reserves. "We can start looking into adopting our girl now."

I contacted America World Adoption Association, and they sent us a short preliminary form. We filled it out and mailed it back.

"Why does the phone *always* ring when I'm in the shower?" I groaned as I wrapped a towel around my dripping body and dashed into our bedroom.

"Hi, Katherine. This is America World."

My heart pounded as the pleasant-sounding receptionist asked, "Are you sitting down?"

Actually, I'm soaking my carpet.

"We have wonderful news for you. You have a match!"

A what? A match? My thoughts spun. *I thought it took months.*

"Oh. Oh, that's wonderful." I finally strung some intelligible sounds together. "I'm just surprised at how fast that was. What's the name?"

"We have a boy for you. Jun."

"Is he …?" I stammered.

"He does have some medical issues," she said. "How about I email you his packet of information, and then you can make an informed decision. Let us know as soon as possible so you can get the paperwork started. That takes some time to complete."

I dashed back to the bathroom to finish my shower. Then I dressed, sat at my computer and clicked on the agency's email. And there he was, lying in a crib, staring up at the camera, his large eyes dark and somber. Fear gripped me as I studied the obvious double cleft lip.

Filled with joy and terror, I punched in Mark's phone number with shaking fingers.

"Let's get as much information as we can before we decide." Mark's calm voice helped settle me.

"Yes, that's a good idea."

We consulted with a doctor who specialized in international adoptions. "Doesn't look good," he said. "From the information here, you're looking at a child who will more than likely be mentally disabled. Severely, based on his current development and head measurements. He'll probably never be able to live independently." He paused. "As a professional, I'd have to advise you not to go forward with this adoption."

I turned to Mark after we'd hung up. "What should we do? We definitely didn't sign up for an adoption such as what the doctor just described."

I called the adoption agency and voiced my concerns.

"We can give you the phone number of a lady who has been to that particular orphanage. She probably met Jun. Why don't you give her a call?"

I dialed the number a few minutes later.

"Hi. This is Katherine. The adoption agency gave me your number and said you probably met the child we're thinking of adopting."

"Probably. What's the name?"

"Jun. Have you met him?"

"A boy! How nice for you. Yes, I've met him. He's quite a cutie."

I gripped the phone with both hands.

This is it. Moment of truth.

"Can you tell me … can you please tell me if he's *in there*?"

"In there? What do you mean?"

"Is he a vegetable?" *Forgive me, God, for even thinking such a thing, but I just have to know.*

"No, certainly not." She laughed. "I've held Jun, and I can assure you that he's 'in there.' His eyes are very bright, and he's quite alert."

I related what the doctor had told us.

"Don't worry about that. He probably felt it was his duty to give you the worst-case scenario to prepare you."

Still, I hesitated. The deadline for our answer came and went. We knew we had to decide one way or the other and let them know.

> "He will not let your foot slip —
> he who watches over you will not slumber."

"Today's the day. We have to give the agency an answer one way or the other."

Mark and I sat down with the telephone between us. He picked up a photo of Jun and studied it.

"I just can't say no," he said.

"Neither can I."

"If we don't say yes, nobody else will. Let's call the agency and tell them we're ready to move forward."

The moment we relayed our decision, I dashed to our bathroom — the only place of guaranteed privacy with three children in the house — and turned the shower water on full blast.

"God," I cried aloud, collapsing on the floor, "if this is your plan for our lives, help us. If you want me to parent this special-needs child, help me to be the best mother I can."

I thought about his medical file, and my fear mounted.

I'm not sure I'm up to the challenge.

I remembered the photo and his large, sad eyes.

He's my son. My son! I realized that the moment I spoke the word "yes," my thoughts and prayers changed from praying for a boy who needed a home to praying for Jun becoming *my son.* Overwhelming love flooded my heart, and I yearned to hold him in my arms.

We have a new son. A son specifically chosen for us from God. But he has huge challenges. How can I take care of him properly?

"I lift up my eyes to the mountains, where does my help come from? My help comes from the Lord …"

I whispered my favorite Psalm to myself over and over until love won and worry vanished.

God, I know you wouldn't put this baby in our path just to have us fail, but I'm going to have to trust you like I've never had to trust you before.

"You'll need a waiver from the Chinese government," the agency explained. "Just because you've said yes to Jun doesn't mean he's yours yet. The government has the final say on all international adoptions."

"The Chinese government could turn us down," I told Mark at dinner, pushing my green beans around on my plate. "Now that I feel Jun is already our son, the government could turn us down."

"Katherine, you've got to relax." Mark laid his own fork down. He reminded me of Proverbs 21: "The king's heart is in the hand of the Lord … he turns it wherever he wishes."

"God is more powerful than the Chinese government," Mark reassured me. "If God wants Jun to be our son, nobody in China — or anywhere else in the world — has the power to stop him."

"I know." I wiped at a tear with the back of my hand. "I wish I could relax in God like you do."

"You worry enough for both of us." Mark raised his water glass and grinned. "That's why I don't bother."

"Thanks, sweetie." I frowned and then smiled.

ॐॐॐ

Is Jun getting enough to eat? Is he cold? Does anybody cuddle him? My baby is thousands of miles away, and there's nothing I can do about it.

Worry swirled in my head until I begged God to take it from me. "He who watches neither slumbers nor sleeps," I repeated to myself.

God, watch over my child when I can't.

"Your waiver arrived." The agency called less than a month later. We knew we needed to brace ourselves. The test of endurance would begin now, with the home study, background checks and loads of paperwork.

❧ ❧ ❧

BOYO-BOYO-BOYO-BOYO.

The noise jolted me from my deep thoughts. I stood staring at the open kitchen cabinet while smoke rose from a skillet on the stove.

"Honey!" Mark dashed into the kitchen. "You've set off the smoke alarm again."

He grabbed a hot pad, tossed the toasted skillet in the sink and shut off the burner's gas. Then he reset the detector.

"Oh, no, not again." Tears rolled down my face as I stared at the charred lumps in the sink. "I was just thinking …"

"I know." He gathered me in his arms and squeezed tight. "Honey, you've got to stop worrying."

"So many questions. What if we don't answer all those questions exactly right? It could hold up the adoption."

"You're doing just fine."

"What about Jun? Is he getting enough to eat? Enough attention?"

"Katherine, don't you think God loves Jun as much as we do?"

"But what if …"

Mark wrapped an arm around me. "Now what does that favorite Psalm of yours tell you about God?"

"The Lord will keep you from all harm. The Lord will watch over your life."

Mark nodded. "He's taking care of Jun, and nothing will stop the adoption if God's in it."

"We're approved!" I almost screamed as Mark walked in the front door. "The agency is putting together a group of adopting parents now. They need to know who is going in our family."

We decided to take our two girls with us and leave Mark Jr. with his granddad. Our group flew to Beijing. We stayed there for two days and then flew on to the capital city of the province where our son lived.

The next morning, the bus transported us — five adopting families — to meet our new sons and daughters. The surrounding mountains took my breath away with their rugged beauty. I marveled at them towering over the city and thought about Psalm 121. "I lift up my eyes to the mountains, where does my help come from? My help comes from the Lord, the maker of heaven and earth."

God, you made these mountains. You sculpted them with your own hand. And you made Jun. And today we get to meet the son you've prepared for us.

We all squeezed into a tiny office in which nannies and other workers from the orphanage stood holding the children. I looked around, but no baby looked like my son. Then, I turned to see our daughters, Alana and Marijane, standing next to one nanny and grinning. They had recognized their pink-pajama-clad brother first.

The nanny placed my new son into my arms and stepped back.

Your head is huge, I thought. I remembered the doctor's report and how much I'd fretted over his assessment that the "head measurement is small for his age." *All those worries for nothing.*

It seemed as if every other baby in the room was bawling, but Jun simply looked at me. I studied his large, expressive eyes and *knew.*

Oh, yes. He's definitely in there.

We named him William, after my father and Mark's father, fulfilling our long-held desire to name our second son after both grandfathers. And then we had to take William Jun to the passport office for photos.

Real terror filled his eyes as he saw buses and autos, crowds of people and sunlight — likely all for the first time in his 27-month-old life.

After we took him back to our hotel room, I noticed that he seemed to be playing peek-a-boo with me. He covered his eyes, looked away, uncovered them and looked back. Each time, his already sad eyes saddened further.

Oh, no! Is he thinking that one of these times when he uncovers his eyes, I'll disappear and he'll be back with his nanny in his own familiar crib?

"All of this hustle and bustle has him over-stimulated," I told Mark and the girls as William Jun seemed to retreat into himself. His obvious terror, wrapped in deafening silence, checked our excited joy. "He's never been around it before. I'm going to put him in a dark room and give him some time to adjust."

After a while, William Jun's fears must have subsided enough for him to fall asleep. Exhausted ourselves, we all piled into our beds and followed his example.

I awakened well before dawn and glanced at my watch.

Oh, dear. William hasn't eaten since before dinner yesterday.

I crept out of bed and rifled through the box of formula. The mixing instructions were in Chinese. I tossed a few scoops into a bottle, added hot water and popped the nipple into his mouth. He sucked it down in seconds, all while still sleeping.

At least I know he's not dehydrated. Relieved, I crawled back into bed.

That morning, we all went downstairs to enjoy the hotel's breakfast buffet. After loading our plates with many fabulous choices, I scooped some soft rice porridge in a spoon and turned to William.

He slapped his hand over his mouth and held it there with determination while terror radiated from his eyes.

"Okay, Jun Jun," I crooned. "I realize this is a bit overwhelming to you. You must be wondering why this complete stranger has you in this strange place, trying to feed you strange food."

I waited until he calmed down a little and tried again.

He flailed at the spoon and hit my arm. Realization sank in.

He might have oral aversion.

Long before our trip to China, I'd read information and blogs from other adoptive parents of Chinese children. One had expressed the difficulty she experienced with her young daughter. She called it oral or feeding aversion.

Many factors can play into oral aversion, such as pain or premature birth — situations that lead to a baby being fed through IV and not the mouth. Even with cleft lip and palate, other babies ate normally for their age, and I thought William would be the same. We soon learned that his lack of exposure to solid foods caused this.

"I'll just give him a bottle of formula when we get back upstairs," I told Mark. But William flipped out again when I brought the nipple close to his mouth. Desperate, I contacted the orphanage to learn how they'd fed him.

"He is used to lying on a flat, hard surface, on his back, and the formula must be boiling hot," our translator said.

I cringed but followed her instructions. William took the bottle. Step by tiny step, I worked toward being able to hold him while eating. First, I sat next to him. This continued for several days. Then, I put one hand under his head as he drank. Then, I ran a hand down his arm. By the end of the week, he allowed me to hold him for the bottle.

Even though he was 27 months old, William's progress was more like that of a 6-month-old. He couldn't sit up by himself for more than a few seconds, and he couldn't stand. He avoided eye contact and remained sensitive to activity around him.

We watched him grieve for the only life he knew and for the nannies, the only people he'd known in his first years of life. It broke our hearts to watch him suffer. I ached to cuddle him and soothe his fears, but he'd have none of that.

"It's so hard not to grab him and hug his sorrow away." I stared at our new son from across the room, forcing myself not to jump up and run to him.

"It's a matter of time," Mark said. "He'll come around. We just have to be patient."

"How you doing, buddy?" A few days later, Mark approached the crib where William lay. "How's Daddy's Jun Jun doing today?"

He reached down and started tickling William's tiny tummy. William grinned. A huge, real, beautiful grin.

We all froze at the sight and then quietly high-fived the progress.

> "The Lord will keep you from all harm —
> he will watch over your life."

Soon after William came to the United States, we met with a team of doctors to prepare for his oral surgery to repair his cleft palate and lip.

"He can't take the bottle after surgery," one doctor informed us.

His words felt like an unpleasant jolt of electricity.

"I don't know what I'll do," I said. "That's the only way we can get any nourishment in him."

"Don't worry," the doctor said. "He'll eat when he's hungry."

"We also ran a test on his hearing," another doctor told us. "He has almost no hearing. We're going to drain his ears and insert tubes at the same time as the palate surgery."

After the surgeries, an occupational therapist gave us a feeding syringe. The therapist seemed to be the only one who actually understood and provided real help and advice, telling us that children with oral aversion are not motivated by hunger. They'd rather starve than allow the thing they fear get close to their mouths, so it took many hours and loads of patience to feed William every day.

We developed games to get him to eat. Just *licking* a spoon took a year. Learning to chew took three.

None of this would be necessary if the orphanage had properly fed my son, I thought. *Why did they keep him on a bottle all that time? Why didn't they introduce him to real food?*

Resentment built as I watched my son struggle to overcome the extreme fear of having anything put into his mouth, day after day, week after week and for months stretching into years.

"The Lord will watch over your coming and going
both now and forevermore."

"Someday, I'd like to go back to the orphanage for a visit," I told Mark.

By that time, both my oldest daughter, Alana, and I were sponsors of other orphans from Q City. We prayed constantly for the children, nannies, director and potential adoptive families.

"Why not now?" Mark checked out our finances. "We can afford it this year."

Alana and I joined another team of people. We planned to shower the children with lots of love and cuddles while demonstrating for the nannies activities that promote healthy development for children with special needs.

Once again, I marveled at the imposing mountains as we descended into Q City. I'd learned that many caves dotted the ravines and that Chinese people had hidden in them during a Japanese invasion. Many people continued to live in those caves, much to my amazement.

Both refuge and risk. People can fall to their death hiking such jagged mountains — or find safety from enemy forces.

After the bus dropped us off at the orphanage where Jun spent the first 27 months of his life, Alana and I gazed around us in amazement. Children played in rooms and were no longer confined to cribs. We heard happy laughter and saw dozens of smiles. In the four years since Jun Jun's adoption, the orphanage had partnered with Love Without Boundaries, which supplied the staff with more training, resources, supplies and teachers for the children.

"Would you like to feed some babies?" asked Violet, our translator.

"Can I?" I asked.

"Absolutely."

A smiling nanny propped up two babies, both with cleft lip and palate like my Jun Jun, and handed me a bowl of noodles. Both children popped their mouths open like baby birds, accepting, chewing and swallowing the food almost faster than I could shovel it into their mouths.

If the nannies had done this for Jun Jun, he wouldn't still have issues, terrified of food because nobody bothered to introduce him to it.

The old, familiar resentment flared up, tainting the overwhelming joy I felt feeding the two babies. Later, I sought the privacy of my hotel room and collapsed onto the bed. Delight from seeing the drastic changes in the orphanage struggled against massive lack of forgiveness toward the nannies.

Oh, God, I cried into the pillow. *Feeding those babies with real food was the greatest gift you could have given me.* I curled my hand around an imaginary spoon. *After all the struggles we've suffered with Jun Jun, to see those babies chewing and swallowing like normal children and enjoying their food took my breath away. Wiping their little mouths. Seeing their little grins. God, I'll never forget this day. Ever.*

I bunched both hands into fists. *If the nannies had*

done this for Jun Jun, he wouldn't have suffered all these years.

It seemed God spoke deep in my heart. *Take a good look at the nannies. Your anger has distorted your ability to see them as I do.*

In that moment, I realized that the nannies were wonderful, loving people, performing service in an unappreciated field. They'd received little to no training on how to care for children with special needs, or of the adverse results from leaving babies lying in cribs all the time and not introducing them to solid foods. I also realized that they did what they could while being short-staffed.

God continued to speak to me. *Don't you realize that what you saw today is the answer to your prayers? These are the changes you prayed for, Katherine. There's always power in prayer.*

Joy flooded my heart. *Lord Jesus, forgive my unbelief! You do more than I can ever ask or imagine.*

"The Lord is your shade at your right hand."

"Would you like to visit the place where William Jun was found?" Violet asked.

"Oh, yes, *yes!*" I said.

The bus took us to another area of town and stopped in front of a building that had previously been the Q City orphanage. The gate guard came out to talk to us.

"What is this building for?" I asked.

"It's being converted to a homeless shelter," Violet explained. "They will call it Salvation Management Station."

How appropriate.

"Do you know what the word salvation means?" I asked Violet. She shook her head. "It means to be rescued. Like the orphanage rescues children. Like God rescues us through Jesus."

"Would you like to see the place where your son was found?" the guard asked.

"You know the exact spot?"

He nodded and led us to an area around the side of the building.

"How can you be sure?" I asked.

"Cameras." He pointed at various areas where security cameras eyed us. "It is illegal to abandon babies in our country. This is the only place a baby could be left without detection."

The guard and Violet moved away as I stood with tears running down my face.

A place of two mamas. Both desperate. One to lay down a son and the other to pick him up.

"God bless her," I prayed in a whisper. "Bless Jun Jun's mama. Only you know the circumstances that made her unable to parent her child. Her desperation and my longing meet on this very spot."

The guard cut a small branch from the nearest tree and gathered some flowers. He placed them in my arms and smiled.

When I returned to the orphanage, a young girl named Lily grabbed my hand and led me to a picture of an American woman holding a Chinese baby.

"Mama," Lily said. Then she pointed to herself.

She wants a mama. Tears welled up in my eyes, and I tried to smile through them.

Next, she led me to a table and showed me her artwork. We spoke the international language of hugs and smiles. Suddenly, she grabbed my hand again and led me out of the room. We walked down several hallways, and she opened the door to a room I hadn't seen before.

Several children gathered around us. Lily signed for me to sing.

I knew no Chinese. These children spoke no English. But as I sang about the love of God through Jesus, their faces glowed. I believe their spirits understood the message I couldn't express in their language.

I felt God's presence pulsating through the room, wrapping the children and me in his holy glory. I sensed his love and pleasure for each one there.

Those considered imperfect and unwanted by others, God sees as perfect and cherished. Mental retardation, cerebral palsy, cleft lip. None of these define the real person. Each child is created in God's image. Their bodies may be less than perfect, but their spirits and souls, emotions and hearts are whole. They have so very much to offer in life.

I carried the awe in my heart as, after many hugs, Lily and I returned to her classroom.

❧❧❧

"This is such a bummer."

Several of us huddled in the director's office after smog delayed our flight out of Q City. Alana, suffering from a stomach virus, was lying down on a cot.

"If we're delayed too long, we're going to miss our flight out of Beijing."

"Yeah. Bummer," another repeated.

"What is that?" I asked Violet, pointing to a large, ornate, red-covered book. She picked it up and looked at the flyleaf.

"Holy Bible," she read.

A Bible? Here?

She began reading the names of different books. We stopped her when she came to the book of John.

"Can you translate it to us from the beginning?" I asked.

"In the … beginning …" She stopped with a frown. "This is really old Chinese. Hard to understand."

"That's okay," we encouraged her. "Just do the best you can."

"In the beginning was the word and the word was with God … and the word … was God" (John 1:1).

She frowned again. "That must be wrong. It doesn't make any sense."

"No, no. That's correct. John is writing about Jesus, God's son, who came to earth as a human."

Violet looked puzzled.

"We call the Bible the word of God because we read about him in it." Again, I pointed to the red book. "But Jesus came to *show us* God. That's why he, too, is called 'the word of God.' Jesus came to show us God's heart."

"He cared about us like we care about the orphans," another team member chimed in. "The orphans didn't know about us. They needed to be rescued. We came to where they were and gave them family. That is what God does for us."

A light came to her eyes.

"Would you like your own Bible?" I asked.

Violet nodded.

Several of us exchanged glances. What did it matter if we missed our flight and got home a day late? Sharing Jesus with Violet was worth it.

"I prayed to God," Violet confided later that day, after a mad dash to make our long-delayed flight. "I prayed you would get here in time." Her eyes widened. "He answered my prayer! I never prayed before, and he answered my prayer."

"Of course. God is always good to his children. Even if we missed *that* flight, we know he'd have a good reason."

"But none of you panicked, either," she said. "That really amazed me. I never saw so many people have so much peace …" She laid a hand over her heart. "In here."

God, you never cease to amaze me. Thank you for showing your love and power to Violet.

❧❧❧

The long flight home gave me plenty of time to think about what I saw and experienced on my second trip to China.

I'm so glad I came. I saw with my own eyes the changes that will keep other orphans from suffering as Jun Jun has. I'm thankful God took all the bitterness from my heart and I can love and appreciate the nannies who work so hard.

I thought about how hard we struggled with William Jun. The cleft lip and palate surgeries seemed like swatting at a pesky gnat next to the challenge of oral aversion. We celebrated each tiny improvement like he had won a marathon.

Was adopting a child with special needs worth the pain? If people never asked me that question directly, I knew they must have thought it.

Absolutely.

I let my mind travel back to Jun Jun's first word. Since joining our family, he'd shown no understanding of spoken communication — until one spring day as several other mothers and I waited outside our church for our children to come from youth group.

"Would you like a taste?" A mom held a lollipop out to William Jun, who was sitting in his stroller.

He turned his head away and covered his mouth.

"Not yet." I stifled a sigh.

"Be patient, Katherine. He'll come around."

"I know. I appreciate your support. I really do."

I pulled a bottle out of my tote bag and handed it to Jun Jun. "Eat," I said, also signing the word.

Jun always grabbed the bottle and chugged down the formula in a few gulps, but that time, he pulled it from his mouth and signed "eat" back to me.

In that moment, we all saw his dark eyes light up with new understanding. Suddenly, he pointed at his stroller, the trees, the grass, his ears and hands, and his shoes and shorts, his mind as starved for words as his body was starved for sufficient nutrition.

᷆᷆᷆

Adopting William Jun gave me new insight to God's heart. Paul wrote, "God destined us to be his adopted children through Jesus Christ because of his love. This was according to his goodwill and plan" (Ephesians 1:4-5 GW).

It took a long time for William Jun to fully trust that we had his best interests at heart through the long struggles of surgery, through learning to walk and talk, and through the long ordeal with oral aversion. For so long, my heart ached with love for my son while his eyes reflected distrust.

We offered him a forever family while watching him grieve for what he'd lost. He rejected our love, our hugs and our concern, longing to return to his familiar past.

I wanted to take away his pain, to dissolve his absolute

terror and to share my heart and love, knowing he wanted no part of it.

All of that gave me a new understanding of God's heart. I realized that God pursues humanity with his perfect love and plans for the best of life. Like Jun, I sometimes reject God's infinite best for my limited perception of best.

This proved especially true during the year we waited for final approval in the adoption. I spent many hours in useless worry. Yet I trust that God never got angry or gave up on me, any more than I could feel anger at Jun Jun's refusal to eat. "God is rich in mercy because of his great love for us" (Ephesians 2:4). I understood how God could remain faithful through my fears and doubts, never wavering in his steadfast love for me.

My relationship with him as my heavenly father has grown as my faith in him has grown. My faith became strong as I found my identity in what Christ has done for me. I am secure in the confidence that his love is too big for anything to separate me from his family into which he's adopted me. I don't have to worry or feel insecure because I'm in Christ — forever.

I marveled at how God seemed to work out all the details — for one Chinese woman to give birth to Jun Jun and to leave him just outside a specific orphanage. And years before Jun's birth, God placed the desire to adopt in our hearts, and in his perfect time, he brought us all together. I realized that's God's relentless love — in action.

RELENTLESS LOVE

"I lift up my eyes to the mountains —
      where does my help come from?
      My help comes from the LORD,
      the Maker of heaven and earth.
      He will not let your foot slip —
he who watches over you will not slumber;
      indeed, he who watches over Israel
      will neither slumber nor sleep.
      The LORD watches over you —
the LORD is your shade at your right hand;
      the sun will not harm you by day,
            nor the moon by night.
The LORD will keep you from all harm —
      he will watch over your life;
the LORD will watch over your coming and going
      both now and forevermore."
            (Psalm 121)

FLY AWAY HOME
The Story of Nicole
Written by Marty Minchin

Two babies, two cribs.

I stared at the tiny wrapped bundles, little cocoons who couldn't be more than a week old, and felt hot tears well in my eyes. There were no rocking chairs in which to sit and hold them, no parents longing to pick up these precious little ones.

"They have been here for two days," our Chinese translator explained in English. "These babies were abandoned, probably outside the gates of the hospital. Before they can go next door to the orphanage, they have to receive a health checkup here."

I longed to pick them up, but we couldn't even go in the door. The babies were in quarantine.

I squinted to try to make out their features, but their cribs were too far toward the back of the room. *Did they have cleft palates? Some other medical condition?*

Why did their mothers leave them?

A profound sadness settled in my heart, as if a boulder were pressing on my chest. I wiped my eyes with the back of my hand, glanced at the babies one more time and followed our tour guide to the next part of the building. I couldn't stop weeping.

꙰꙰꙰

I was born 12 weeks premature in Spokane, Washington. While I was rushed to the NICU, my mom, who had developed an infection, stayed in the intensive care unit while Dad shuttled between our rooms. Miraculously, I was taken off the respirator after two days, but my parents couldn't take me home for another six weeks.

My mom gave birth to my sister, Lara, 18 months later. Eighteen months after that, she walked out on my dad to be with another man, leaving my sister and me behind.

Dad was devastated. A young man in his 20s with two little girls, Dad had thrived on rescuing broken people like my mom, but now he needed rescuing himself. He called me his "lifeboat," and while he provided for Lara and me, he depended on our young ears to listen and leaned on us emotionally for support.

We didn't hear from Mom for about a year. By then, I was almost 4 years old, and my dad had met Kate, who had a son just two weeks older than my sister.

My memories of Mom are vague. She moved to California with a guy, and I remember flying on a plane by myself at a very young age to visit her. Sometimes, Lara and I would spend part of a holiday with her, but Mom drank — a lot — and spewed horrible words about my dad. We couldn't wait to leave.

By contrast, Kate possessed a kind, calming nature.

Unfortunately, Dad didn't always keep his emotions in check. They floated near the surface, and when Dad would storm out of the house during a fight, he'd often slam a door or declare, "Let's just get divorced!" But Kate stayed, and she became a mother to us as much as she could.

Our cobbled-together family blew around with the wind. I attended 13 schools between kindergarten and 12th grade. We moved for Dad's job or Kate's job or Kate's schooling to become a nurse midwife. By the time I got to college, the apartment I rented as an undergrad became the place I'd lived the longest.

My college friends thought it would be a good idea for me to go out to pizza with them and meet a guy they believed was a good match. I was leaving town the next day, so I initially turned down the invitation.

"No, really, you should come," my friend prodded. "You need to meet him."

So I went, and I met Daniel. He was a good five inches shorter than I was.

My friends had teased him about his height before introducing us. "How desperate are you?" they asked. "She's kind of taller than you."

"How tall? Amazon tall?"

"Well, kind of."

Despite our height difference, Daniel and I hit it off immediately. He was funny, charming, witty and very "civil engineer-ish," as I like to say, and he proceeded with our courtship very precisely. We held hands after one month of dating, kissed for the first time on our six-month anniversary and got engaged exactly one year after we met. We honeymooned in Maui and met another couple with the same professional pairing as us — a nurse and a civil engineer. Medical professionals and engineers must be unusually compatible, we thought.

Daniel and I talked about having kids, but those conversations were more abstract discussions than plans for an immediate reality. However, we both wanted kids.

"Would you ever be interested in adoption?" I asked. I'd long seen myself adopting a child one day. Giving a child a stable home was appealing — I knew exactly what it was like to live in chaos and uncertainty.

"Yeah, maybe," Daniel replied.

Good enough.

తతత

My Christian faith developed in leaps and bounds in my 20s. Daniel was the son of a preacher, and we became involved in our church and sought God's will for our lives. I began a career as a nurse practitioner, following a longtime dream of working in the medical field. I wanted to help other people, and when our church offered an opportunity to go on a medical mission trip to Costa Rica, I jumped at the chance. We treated large families — kids, parents, grandparents — who came for checkups. I later went on a similar trip to Nicaragua.

My own family at home was growing. Andrew was born in 2008, and his little brother, Alex, joined us in

2012. When I took Alex to the doctor for his 11-month checkup, the pediatrician furrowed his brow and told me that my baby hadn't gained any weight in two months. Alex had a hard time keeping anything down, so much so that whenever we gave him a bottle, we covered ourselves with a blanket first.

After a barrage of tests and appointments with specialists, he was diagnosed with a condition that inflamed his esophagus, made swallowing difficult and gave him a hyperimmune response to many foods. In real life, that meant we had to thicken all his liquids, give him six medications a day and remove everything from wheat to bananas from his diet. We were soon on a first-name basis with the staff at the children's hospital, which — thank God — was only five minutes from our house. I began calling Alex my "ER child."

In the midst of our struggles with Alex's health, my friend Sandy asked me to pray about going with her on a mission trip to China.

"We'll be serving at an orphanage," she explained. "Foreigners rarely visit, and we can help by getting to know the kids and helping the Chinese caregivers. We'll also help update information on the kids' files for potential adoptive families."

Never in a million years had I considered going to China, but I knew that Sandy had prayed about whether to approach me with an invitation for the trip. So I did pray, and I talked to my friends about the trip and asked for their advice.

It wasn't an ideal time. I had a job at the hospital, and 18-month-old Alex required a lot of care and attention. The more I talked and prayed, however, the more I felt a great peace enveloping me. I decided to go to China, even though I had no idea why God might want me there.

First, each member of our team needed to raise about $4,000 to pay for the flight and other expenses. The first time I'd gone on a mission trip, I paid my own way. For the second mission trip, we'd had the money before car trouble sucked it away. I'd had to write letters asking for money, and the whole process felt awkward.

Daniel and I couldn't contribute toward the trip to China, and this time the amount I needed was double the cost of my other trips.

Trust me with your finances, I felt God tell me.

I raised $4,200, and together our team collected $10,000 more than we needed for the trip. In October 2014, I boarded a plane for China.

My world has never been the same since.

స్థ స్థ స్థ

The plane touched down in the middle of the night in Beijing. I pressed my face to the window, marveling at the rows and rows of lights illuminating the huge airport.

Somehow, our plane was the only one disembarking, and our group walked through cavernous, fluorescent-lit hallways to customs and got in the line marked "Foreigners" in Mandarin and English.

Nothing around me was familiar. I could understand a little of the Spanish spoken in Costa Rica and Nicaragua, but the Chinese tones were gibberish to me. I couldn't read the Chinese characters on the signs, and I was grateful for the occasional English translation.

My group filled half the manifest on our commuter flight the next morning to the rural town of Q City. The director of the orphanage was waiting for us at the tiny airport, a huge smile on his face as he greeted the first Americans to visit in several years.

My friend Stacy already had tears in her eyes as we settled into the back seat of the orphanage director's car.

"Do you remember me?" she asked. "I was here a few years ago to pick up my little girl, Li Na." Our translator spoke Stacy's words in Mandarin for the director, who sat in the front seat with the driver.

Stacy pulled out a stack of pictures from her purse and passed them to the director as if he were a grandparent eager to see photos of his grandchildren.

"Look how big she is now!" Stacy said. "She is such a blessing to our family." She leaned over the seat and watched as the director thumbed through the pictures, the smile never leaving his face. It was clear how much he cared about the children at his orphanage.

"I remember her," he spoke through the translator. "She looks like she has a happy life with your family. Why did you come back? This is a long way for you to travel."

Stacy grinned. "I am so thankful for my daughter, Li Na. I wanted to help more at her orphanage."

Our caravan of vehicles stopped in front of the orphanage's complex, which included a small hospital emblazoned with huge red Chinese characters.

"No pictures," the translators told our group before we went inside. "Also, you cannot talk to anyone about religion and politics. You should focus your conversations on the children."

I felt for my phone in my purse, wishing I could pull it out and snap pictures. We needed to advocate for these children, and pictures would help potential adopters build a connection with them. I wondered, with all of these rules, if the orphanage would accept all the toys we had brought in our suitcases.

My eyes moistened, and they were still wet as we left the hospital. I couldn't stop thinking about those two babies, all alone, with no parents to love them.

Could I handle a whole orphanage full of children, many abandoned just like me?

శశశ

Chinese parents leave their babies for many reasons. Culture dictates that children should one day take care of their parents, and a child with a disability may not be able to do that.

Some parents don't have the resources to get treatment for children with disabilities or diseases.

I imagined the mother of each of these precious children facing the unfathomable decision of keeping or giving away her baby. Those women must yearn for their lost children, wondering what they were like, how they were doing.

The orphanage was our next stop after the hospital.

As we pushed open the door to the older children's schoolroom, a sea of smiles greeted us.

I noticed a number of medical conditions right away, including Down syndrome and cerebral palsy.

The teacher commanded her class' attention, and the students dutifully lined up in front of the classroom to recite a poem for us in Mandarin. Then the children tumbled out of formation, eager to meet the strangers visiting their class.

One child, whom I nicknamed John, limped straight to me and grabbed my hand. A condition — probably mild cerebral palsy — had left one of his legs in a brace, but that didn't slow him down.

I smiled at him. "Hi, I'm Nicole."

John seemed in no hurry to let go of my hand, so we walked around the room together to greet his classmates. The students, all between ages 8 and 21, were as porous as sponges, soaking up any touch, any hug they could get. When it was time to move on to the next room, I gently led John to his desk.

"I'll see you soon, buddy," I assured him.

The next room, Baby Room 2, housed toddlers. Wooden cribs outfitted with bright pink mattresses lined the white walls. Many of the cribs held young children. A few were pushed around the floor in wheeled walkers.

While the older children's room was full of light and smiles, the baby rooms were incredibly quiet.

No pictures could have prepared me for Baby Room 1.

Once again, cribs filled the room, with each crib holding an infant. It was feeding time — a regimented process. The Chinese nanny pushed around a bin of bottles and gave one bottle to each baby. Tiny popping sounds filled the room as they sucked, some choking on the milk. When feeding time was over, the nanny made another round and collected the bottles, regardless of whether the babies were finished eating.

"They get four bottles a day," the translator told us.

What? I was shocked. A newborn needs to eat every two hours. I walked around the room, marveling at the silence. Some of the bottles were still half full of milk when they were collected. These babies had to be hungry still. I peered at the tiny faces, noting that many of them had obvious cleft palates or lips.

It was difficult to determine why some kids were in the orphanage, and it was heartbreaking to realize that many of the problems the others had could have been easily corrected. Surgery could fix a cleft palate and misshapen mouth. Kids suffering from severe hydrocephalus, with skulls so heavy they couldn't lift their heads, could have received a shunt to drain the extra fluid. We wondered if life in an orphanage had slowed some kids' development, creating significant problems that wouldn't have existed if they'd been with a family.

The clean white walls of Baby Room 2 would become

the destination for kids with the most severe problems. As they aged, they'd become unadoptable and likely would never leave the orphanage.

❧❧❧

"We need to get these kids out," our team leader, Charlotte, told us as we ate breakfast at the hotel the next morning. "I don't mean out of the orphanage right now, but out of those cribs. Outside to play. The nannies love these kids, but they worry too much that taking them out will hurt them. Plus, the nannies are so overwhelmed with feeding and laundry and changing so many kids that they may not have time for much else."

I was assigned to Baby Room 1 for the first shift that day. The babies had already eaten when we arrived, so I could see their faces without bottles in front of them. Many were sleeping, but we lifted the ones who were awake out of the cribs, snuggling them close. We sang softly to them and patted them when they cried. A few kept wailing, and I wondered if they were uncomfortable or in pain.

As I set out on another round to see which babies may be awake, I stopped short in front of a crib. A tiny baby looked back at me with clear black eyes and a wrinkly forehead, like an old woman noticing everything. She was as still as a mouse.

"Who are you?" I murmured, reaching down to pick her up.

Her upper lip was cleft, creating a large cavity with pink gums showing. Her stare was intense, and she slowly turned her head to look at the world outside her crib.

"You're a tiny little thing, aren't you?" I whispered to her, smoothing the tiny wisps of black hair on her nearly bald head. "How long have you been in there?"

Zhang Jing, I learned, was about 6 weeks old and had been abandoned at the hospital when she was 3 days old. She was the most alert baby I'd ever seen. I settled her into the crook of my arm and fed her with a special bottle nipple we'd brought for cleft babies, who can have trouble sucking conventional nipples. When the nannies signaled that feeding time was over, I held her tightly, telling them she needed more time to finish.

Whenever I could, I carried Zhang Jing in my arms for as many hours as the nannies would allow. I put her on her tummy to test her arm strength and played with her whenever I could. Anything to get her out of the crib and close to me. My team members would switch shifts with me often so that I could maximize my time in Baby Room 1 with Zhang Jing. They knew I was smitten with her.

I gave her an American name, calling her Claire. Daniel didn't want any more kids — he'd had a vasectomy after Alex was born — but if we'd had a girl, Claire would have been her name. Soon all of my team members were calling her Claire, too.

As I walked around with Claire, I prayed for her. By Wednesday, my prayers for her future family took a new turn.

God, I prayed, *are we her future family? Did you bring me to China to meet this little girl?*

My mind flirted with the possibility. In my head, I began to rearrange my house, with the boys bunking up so Claire could have a nursery. I figured out how I could manage my work schedule at the hospital with a new baby at home.

That evening, the entire team squished into one hotel room for worship, prayer and a discussion of our day at the orphanage.

Four of us stayed later to pray about whether God was calling us to adopt: "God, is this what you would have us do? Are these precious children meant to be our children? Please give us direction. Show us your will for our lives and our families."

そうそうそう

On Thursday, I emailed Daniel a picture of Claire. We had tried to Skype every day, but the 13-hour time difference made it difficult.

"Look at this little girl I met," I typed into the message field. "What do you think about her?"

"She looks nice. Cute blue shirt," he responded.

I sent more pictures, some of me smiling with Claire in my arms, using my phone from a hot spot a team member had set up. It wasn't appropriate for us to have a big conversation about adoption with me half a world away, so pictures would have to do for the moment. When I was leaving the United States, Daniel's mother had remarked, "Chubby one, skinny one, boy or girl — all of them are fine with me." Daniel knew why I was sending him those pictures. I wanted Claire to be our daughter.

ൟൟൟ

On Friday, I sat in a rocking chair with Claire and sobbed, my tears falling on her face and head. I snuggled my face into her neck, trying to memorize every touch, every smell, every sight of her.

God, keep this baby safe. Help her to grow and thrive, to be cherished by a Christian family, whether or not that family is us. Bless her with good health, and let her always know that she is loved.

This baby had no one to fight for her, no one to advocate for her. Without surgery to correct her cleft lip and palate, I feared she'd grow up an outcast.

I know you love the "least of these," God. Claire doesn't have a mom and a dad to watch out for her. Protect her.

I wrapped Claire in a little blanket that I'd made before I left for China. We'd put together a number of sensory blankets that had tags of ribbon for babies to touch and feel sewn around the edges. This particular blanket was special because I'd made it using a scrap of purple ribbon that my mother-in-law had given me. One of the nannies had written "Zhang Jing" on it in Chinese characters, and I hoped that when I left it would stay with her, a reminder of these five days in which I sought to show her as much love as I possibly could.

"I'll see you again," I whispered, laying Claire in her crib. "I love you."

I was absolutely convinced that this baby was going to be my daughter.

❧❧❧

Daniel and I sat at the kitchen table to talk not long after I got home. I'd mentioned Claire many times when telling him and the boys about my trip, but the word "adoption" hadn't come up. Daniel hadn't asked much about Claire, either.

"So, this baby that I sent you all of the pictures of," I began, testing the waters. His responses to my emails had been noncommittal, and I wasn't sure where he stood.

"Yeah, I saw them."

"Well, what did you think?"

"She looks like a nice baby."

"I've been praying a lot about her since I left. Actually, I started praying about her, and for her, when I was there. It's incredible what kind of bond you can form with a baby in a really short time."

"Uh-huh."

"I started to call her Claire — you know, the name we planned to give Alex if he'd been a girl. I spent as much time with her as I could, and she just captured my heart. I can't even explain how much I fell in love with her. Seeing

CRADLES IN Q CITY

all those babies in that orphanage made God's command to love orphans so *real.* I really saw why God talks about it so much in the Bible. And then I felt like God was calling me to love her. I sensed really strongly that we are supposed to adopt her."

I searched Daniel's face for any kind of response. He looked down at the table at his clasped hands.

"I don't know, Nicole," he said slowly. "I don't feel that way at all. I'm pretty happy with the two we have. Our family feels complete. Plus, Alex has a lot of medical issues. I don't think we need to take on another kid who's going to be in and out of the hospital. That's a lot to take on. Too much for us."

Daniel might as well have grabbed my heart with both hands and twisted. Couldn't he see how much I loved Claire and how certain I was that she was the reason I went to China?

"Are you sure?" I couldn't let this be the final word. "We could pray about it together and keep talking another time."

"I'm positive, Nicole. Two kids are enough."

ࡄࡄࡄ

While Daniel could brush aside adoption, I couldn't. I looked at Claire's pictures on my phone every day and smiled at her image on the screen.

I fell before God like a broken marionette.

Why would you put something so specific on my heart

and not give Daniel the same vision? I prayed. *He's as strongly against adopting Claire as I am for it. What are you trying to teach us through this?*

Answers were sparse while questions abounded. Sometimes conversations became too painful, so Daniel and I stopped talking about adoption. He said that while he was glad for the passion I had for adoption, he hadn't been to China and hadn't felt what I'd felt. I tried going to counseling, but I couldn't get Daniel to go with me. The issue between us became the elephant in the room, always there but never discussed.

Meanwhile, everyone around us seemed to be having babies or adopting children. One by one, the three people who prayed with me in the Chinese hotel room set the process in motion to bring home children from China. Other friends became pregnant. I smiled and rejoiced with them, but bitterness entered my heart.

Why am I left out? I see your handprint on every adoption. What about me?

My co-workers at the hospital tried to reassure me. I loved telling them the amazing stories of my friends' adoptions, but underneath the joy was sadness that my own adoption story wasn't being written. "Your time will come, don't worry," they'd say. But would it? I asked God every day to protect Claire and to change Daniel's heart.

❧❧❧

The following October, a year after I met Claire, several members of my team traveled back to the orphanage in Q City. I couldn't go along, but I begged for pictures of my sweet girl. I'd learned that she'd been selected for surgery to have her cleft lip repaired.

"Give her tons of hugs and kisses for me," I told them.

The pictures they sent me showed a serious 1-year-old, her upper lip expertly sewn together. My team worked hard to make her smile, and she had a beautiful grin on her face in a few pictures. They took a video of her eating puff chips for the first time, and I marveled at how much she'd grown and changed.

The longing to adopt Claire flared up anew. I ached to hold Claire and make her part of our family. Daniel stood firm on his position, though, refusing to entertain the idea of adoption.

These pictures, I finally admitted, were of someone else's daughter. With her palate corrected, it would only be a matter of time before Claire would be matched with a family. Secretly, part of me still hoped God might move mightily before then, if Daniel and I were supposed to be her parents.

As Daniel was reading a book to the boys on our iPad one night in January, I sent him a message: "I need you to come out here now."

Daniel found me looking down at my phone, staring blankly at a text from a friend. "This isn't public yet, but Claire's been matched with a family."

I dropped my head and sobbed as Daniel hugged me.

My tears lasted for three hours as I came to terms with what I knew was inevitable. Any hope that a miracle would change the circumstances had been squashed.

God spoke to my heart over the next few days as I struggled to untangle my emotions.

You've made adoption an idol.

It was true. Adopting Claire had become more important to me than following God.

This is why you grieve so much, I sensed God telling me. *Will you let me be the one who satisfies you and brings you joy now?*

For so long, my single thought had been, "If I can just adopt her, I'll be happy." I'd wrestled with my anger and discontent for almost a year, putting all my hopes into God making my dreams of adoption come true.

Then, answers began unfolding, and I began to understand that God was working mightily through my trip to China.

I believe God did send me to China to meet Claire and to pray for her. But not so that I would adopt her. I came to understand that he needed me to gather pictures and stories — for her future mother and father.

She is going to be safe, God whispered to me gently. *Can I be enough? No matter what you went through as a child, no matter how healthy your children are, no matter what the state of your marriage, can you find satisfaction in me?*

Yes.

আপ আপ আপ

I had one more gift for Zhang Jing and her new family, who live in the Pacific Northwest. I pulled out all the pictures of my girl, of me loving on her, and made them into a baby book. I showed her parents before and after pictures of her cleft lip and photos of the wonderful Chinese nannies who loved her the best they could. I shared pictures taken around the town of Q City. I wrote what I knew of her story next to the photos.

Then, I opened my heart and wrote them a letter on the last page.

I have prayed for her forever family since the day I met her. I prayed for a family that would treasure and adore her. I have prayed for her safety, prayed for her growth, prayed over her resting and her waking. I've prayed for her story to point to Jesus. I've prayed for her salvation. I've prayed for you both without even knowing who you were. I prayed for peace in your hearts as you started this journey.

We may never meet, but know that I am continuing to pray over you as you count down the days until you meet your daughter. I will always pray for Zhang Jing. God forever changed my heart by bringing her into my life, and for that, I will always be grateful.

Xie, Zhang Jing
I love you,
Nicole

FROM HELL TO HOPE
The Story of Joel
Written by Sharon Kirk Clifton

The subway train stopped. Strange. We'd just passed the 14th Street station, where much of the rush-hour crowd had disembarked. We weren't due to stop again for a while. I knew this route well. I should. I traveled it every weekday to and from the Brooklyn courthouse where I worked.

I hoped that whatever was going on didn't delay us long. Family court was my beat. Like every weekday, I had a burden of cases to sort through with disgruntled parents and grandparents, trying to pacify them as they fought like feral cats over the custody and support of their children or grandchildren.

Suddenly, we were plunged into utter darkness. Palpable darkness. The kind I didn't just see. I felt it pressing in on me, threatening to cut off my oxygen supply.

Everyone fell silent — waiting, listening for a creaking noise or the sound of metal on metal, anything that might hint of movement.

We sat or stood in our normal compressed state for a half hour. Eventually, a low rumble of voices began as people speculated about why we'd stopped.

Finally, the safety lights came on, about every 50 feet.

The doors on one side of the cars opened, and subway workers in orange and white vests shouted orders.

"Everybody! Everybody! Start moving in this direction. We're going to get off the train. Now!" Still, no one told us why. People were calm and somber. We just kept walking and walking through car after car after car. Soon, we realized this was more than just our train. This was many trains put together. Eventually, we reached the end. We got off the last train car and walked along the tracks for about 100 yards more.

Still no one would say what was going on. It was surreal. We moved in silence, herded toward the exit where thick clouds of smoke and dust billowed in from the outside.

If we hesitated, the workers yelled at us.

"Keep it moving, folks. Keep walking. Quickly! Quickly!"

Inside me, a vague fear grew.

When we got to street level, I could barely see. Acrid smoke burned my lungs and coated my mouth and throat.

Good thing Marie's not here. My wife suffered from severe breathing problems.

What I wouldn't give for a bottle of cold water right now.

The air pulsated with the deafening sound of converging sirens. I looked toward the World Trade Center, expecting to see two towers but seeing only one.

What the hell's going on? Where's the other tower?

On the train ride from my home in White Plains to

Grand Central Station, I'd overheard someone say something about a plane hitting one of the towers. I'd assumed it had been a small private plane. That wouldn't have caused this level of destruction, though.

Workers outside the subway directed us further.

"Keep walking uptown. Keep walking uptown."

I got a few feet away from the subway station and stood in the Federal Plaza. It barely resembled the beautiful plaza I knew so well. A layer of gray ash coated the early-autumn blush of the tree leaves. Buildings stood like spectral sentinels guarding the devastation. People, their faces dazed and expressionless, their clothes torn — and in many cases, blood-splattered — ran or limped. Women approached barefoot, having cast aside their high heels to facilitate running.

I looked up and saw shadows falling from the sky. *What were they?* I couldn't tell. Later, I learned they were people falling — people who perhaps chose to die quickly rather than be burned alive.

As I stared transfixed at the lone tower, watching black smoke billow from its upper levels, I heard an unearthly roar grow and watched as the building slowly crumbled to the ground, as if it had imploded. The collapse, mingled with the screams of people and the wail of sirens, was deafening. I'd never heard anything so loud. I clapped my hands over my ears.

Get away! Get away from this! I took off running with the crowd. *Get away! Faster! Don't get caught in the confusion.*

When I'd put some distance between myself and the tumult, I tried to call Marie to let her know I was okay. Around me, people with cellphones couldn't get reception. I found a pay phone but couldn't get through. Then I called a friend in Pennsylvania. Maybe someone outside the immediate area could tell me what was going on.

"I think I just saw one of the WTC towers fall." I could hear the panic in my own voice, as I screamed at the mouthpiece to be heard above the chaos around me. "I think the other one's already gone."

"Yeah. The whole world saw it. They crashed two jetliners into the towers." Then he told me about the Pentagon and the one plane that was diverted in Pennsylvania, near where he lived.

"They weren't accidents," I realized.

"No, Joel, they weren't accidents."

We were under attack. Who would do such a heinous thing? The Cold War had been over for a decade.

I hung up and pushed on toward Grand Central Station, about 40 blocks away. Every once in a while, jet fighters flew overhead. When I heard them, I ducked into a building lobby and waited for them to pass. It sounded as though we were at war.

Once home, I got a cold beer and watched TV news coverage. My friend called to let me know he'd managed to contact Marie and tell her I was okay.

That evening, she told me about her day. Being a pediatrician, she was called to an area hospital where they expected many wounded to be brought. It was an odd situation, though — very few came. Most either died in the attack or escaped.

I couldn't go back to work for a month. Anger consumed me — anger at the terrorists, anger that I'd had to witness the aftermath of the attack. But most of all, anger at God. How could I possibly reconcile the devastation and carnage I'd seen with a loving God? Where was God in all this? I'd been a good Catholic all my life, faithful to Mass, faithful to the sacraments, faithful to my marriage vows. Yet there I was, questioning God. Why hadn't he somehow thwarted the terrorists' plans? Could I ever trust him again?

I felt like I'd glimpsed hell itself.

❧❧❧

I was a law clerk for a family court judge in Brooklyn. When I first began working with that judge, we'd dealt with civil court and regular trials. Then, he made a political deal to work family court. That wasn't what I wanted to do, considering how badly my wife and I wanted to have children and couldn't. My job required that I help settle disputes of people playing tug-of-war with their kids. It made me sick. Each day, I met with 30 separate groups of people disputing child custody. My job was to try to come to a solution pleasing to all parties so that the judge wouldn't have to hear the case. That way, they hopefully would get something close to what they wanted instead of what the judge decided.

A month after 9/11, still suffering emotional trauma, I forced myself back to work, all the while seeking another position. I struggled through six more months until I landed a job with an appeals court.

ॐॐॐ

Marie and I had known since 1998 that we could not have children naturally. The news had devastated us. Artificial insemination was our only option, doctors informed us, but that would violate our Catholic faith. We considered adoption, but learned that, in the United States, domestic adoption was a long, arduous process cluttered with many hoops to jump through and requiring compromises between the parties involved. International adoption usually delivered a child into the adoptive parents' arms faster, so we decided to go that route. After researching adoption procedures for several countries, we settled on China.

Most of the orphans in China were true orphans, children abandoned by their parents. In most cases, the parents couldn't be found. The orphans were in government facilities, and when we applied, China encouraged adoption. They required no back-and-forth bonding visits with the child before adoptive parents picked up their child. At that time, most of the children available for adoption were girls or children with special needs.

We began the application process in June 2002, nine

months after the WTC attack. I say "we," but Marie was minimally involved because she suffered greatly from her breathing problems while continuing to practice medicine full time. She had been born prematurely, and her lungs never developed properly.

Though China's application procedures were not as complicated as those of other countries, they still required reams of paperwork, multiple background checks and fingerprinting at various governmental levels, home visits and inspections, photographs and translation into Chinese. We chose to go through an agency run by a Catholic group out of Massachusetts. They had people in New York who helped me through the process.

A bitter root of anger against God that had begun growing that day in September 2001 continued to flourish. I still believed in God, but I didn't believe in his love. I couldn't see his involvement in our lives. As it was, *I* had to bear the burden of the adoption work myself. *I* had to make sure everything was done to meet deadlines. *I* had to fill out the paperwork, lick the stamps, make the right contacts. *I* did it. Through the grumbling, I was proud of what *I* was accomplishing. *I*, not God.

❧❧❧

The late June day we received three photographs of our little girl, our Zoe, was like Christmas. She was so cute, with her blue-black hair and chubby cheeks. She looked healthy but sad. So sad.

CRADLES IN Q CITY

Along with the pictures, the adoption agency sent information about her personality. We laughed when we read, "She makes more noise than other children." They said we could get her in July.

Then the SARS epidemic — a viral respiratory illness — hit China hard. On TV, we saw people wearing surgical masks as they went about their daily business. The government of China put adoptions on hold for two months.

Those two months were miserable. However, it turned out to be a good thing we hadn't left for China when originally intended because Marie's health took a bad turn. Her doctor put her on strong steroids that caused her body to blow up like a marshmallow. She had to take off work for a month to be stabilized before our anticipated trip to China. We finally got word that we could go in September to claim our Zoe. By then, Marie was better.

We flew to Beijing and did some sightseeing of the Forbidden City and the Great Wall before traveling to the province where our girl awaited. In 2003, the city air was still relatively clean and people got around on bicycles. Everywhere we went, we saw people wearing gray Mao uniforms.

After the three-hour flight from Beijing to Hefei, our guide met us and took us to our hotel, a Holiday Inn, where many Americans stayed.

Our room smelled like a stale ashtray, and cigarette burns marred furniture. Smoke-free rooms were a foreign concept in China, where it seemed everyone chain-smoked.

"Look at that." Marie pointed toward a little wooden crib held together with rope against one wall. "Joel, that's a death trap!"

We'd brought along a duffel bag stuffed with baby-girl clothes, toys, diapers, blankets and other supplies. Marie yanked the blankets out and covered every surface of the death trap.

"There is no way under heaven I'm going to let our daughter come in contact with any part of that contraption."

"Should I go shopping for a large inflatable bubble to put her in?" I asked.

She whirled around, arms akimbo and wearing a sarcastic grin. "If you can find one, that would be a great idea, Mr. Hotshot."

It amazed me how quickly Marie transformed into Super Mom. Or Super Mama Bear, protecting her young.

Our time in China was hard on Marie because of the tobacco smoke. Although she was on strong medications to control her breathing, she still had to keep an inhaler handy. We wanted to get Zoe and head home as soon as possible, but it still took time.

Across from the hotel was a beautiful park with a lake. We needed the fresh air, so we decided to take a walk. A fence surrounded the park, and we had to pay to get in. Although Beijing hosted many tourists, Hefei didn't, so we were something of a novelty. Everyone we passed turned to stare at us unabashedly. College-age students hurried over to us, blocking our path so we had to stop.

"Hello," they said in stilted English. "How are you?"

We tried to answer in Chinese as best we could.

"No, no. Speak in English. English, please."

They wanted to practice on us.

Our guide, Xiao, returned the next morning to escort us to another hotel, where we would receive Zoe. Then I had trouble breathing, from the excitement of finally meeting our daughter. We joined about 20 other couples from all over the world in a ballroom, where we waited for two hours with nothing to do but make small talk and stare at one another. The room was too hot.

Finally, we heard a commotion in the hallway. The doors opened, and we saw about 30 children accompanied by 10 nannies. Our excitement grew. Xiao went to get Zoe and the nanny who was with her. Our girl looked enough like her photos that we recognized her, but in the three months we'd waited, she'd lost a lot of weight. In fact, all the children looked malnourished.

The children were overdressed. Even though it was summer, they were wearing so many layers that they could barely move. Since the ballroom was hot, Marie began removing Zoe's layers as if she were peeling an onion. Finally, she got down to one layer over Zoe's little torso.

Concern flashed across her face. "Joel, feel her ribs."

Zoe definitely was too skinny. At 11 months old, she should have had a layer of baby pudge.

"Well, little girl, we'll just have to feed you some good

food." I tried to hug her, but she pushed me away and started crying. By the time we left the ballroom, all the children were crying. Poor little ones. Most of them had no idea what was going on, nor could they understand a word we said. As soon as we were free to go, we left.

We came to a fountain in the hotel lobby and stopped long enough for Zoe to splash her hands in the water. That stopped her tears.

The taxi driver who transported us to the hotel insisted that Zoe sit up front with Marie, who protested, "No. That's not safe. She has to be in her car seat and buckled in."

The driver didn't understand, or at least he pretended not to. Zoe ended up in front with Marie, who held her securely on her lap while praying for no abrupt stops.

Suddenly, Zoe started laughing. At first, we couldn't figure out why, but then she leaned toward the door and laughed harder.

Then Marie laughed, too. "It's the wind, Joel. Is it possible she's never felt the wind on her face like this? She loves it."

Later that day, we took her for a walk in the park. Older women hurried over to us, scowling and shouting angrily. We finally figured out they were scolding us for not having enough layers on Zoe. Judging by their frantic gestures, they were telling us she'd get sick if we didn't get her bundled up.

Although we were eager to return home, more paperwork remained. Xiao took care of many details, and then we traveled to the American Consulate in Guangzhou. After we waded through more red tape, Zoe had another medical exam in order to get her visa before finally being sworn in as a U.S. citizen at the consulate.

Guangzhou was a beautiful tropical city. While we were there, we stayed at the Swan Hotel, and Zoe experienced a swimming pool for the first time in her life. She definitely loved being in the water.

At long last, we flew home. Our first stop was Chicago, where we got papers declaring Zoe a citizen of the United States of America. Then we continued on to New York, where family and friends waited to greet us and welcome the newest member of our family.

ॐॐॐ

Marie's health worsened, but the doctors couldn't pinpoint exactly what was causing her problems. She had surgery to remove a part of her lung that was diseased. Then, about 18 months after we got Zoe, we went to Washington, D.C.'s National Institute of Health, where Marie spent a day undergoing evaluations and tests. The doctors didn't arrive at any conclusions, but they put her on a strong regimen of antibiotics and told us that she'd be on them long-term, possibly for the rest of her life. The medications stabilized her enough that we could consider adopting a second child from China.

I was a pro at filling out the paperwork the second time around. I got it all done in record time and submitted it to the same agency we'd used for Zoe, who was ecstatic at the idea of having a baby sister.

We didn't hear anything from the agency for several months. Then we got a letter stating that the agency had changed names and was no longer affiliated with the Catholic church. We decided to stick with them, anyway, since they'd gotten us through the process with Zoe. This time, nothing went smoothly. They misplaced our paperwork, so it didn't make it to China for many additional months. By that time, a major earthquake had struck China, which further slowed the works. Then Chinese leaders began to recognize a growing imbalance of girls and boys in their culture. Whom were the boys supposed to marry once they reached adulthood? In an effort to rectify the balance, they began a campaign to urge Chinese people to adopt healthy girls. The wait time for foreigners like us kept getting longer and longer.

One group of children was still available for adoption — those with special needs. Marie and I sat down over coffee to discuss the possibility.

"What do you think?" I said. "Are you willing to accept a special-needs child?"

She took a slow sip from her cup before answering. "It would depend on what the needs were."

"Like?"

"Joel, I can't be a stay-at-home mom. I love my work. What I do is important. And if I'm not there to serve my demographic, I'm not sure who will."

I understood where she was coming from. She worked

at a clinic in a wealthy community, which also contained a large number of immigrants who worked in the homes of the wealthy people. The immigrants came to my wife's clinic, and she had a close connection with the children. Further, she spoke Spanish, which helped. She felt God had put her in that position for a reason.

"I can't just walk away," she said.

"So what do we do?"

"Not all special-needs kids require full-time, hands-on care. Let's see what's available."

Our agency kept sending us pictures of children that we decided we couldn't take. It broke my heart to see them, because I understood that they needed loving parents to take them. But we could not consider children who needed 24/7 nursing care.

Then we got still shots and a two-minute video of one little girl. We read her story. She was missing part of a lung. Just like Marie.

Coincidence? Or was God actually getting involved at a personal level?

During this time, I was mending my relationship with God. I'd begun reading my Bible and spending time trying to understand God's mysterious ways.

After reading this child's medical report, we prayed about her. *All right, God. Is this the one?*

We both strongly felt she was for us. Lian was nearly 2 years old when we went to China to get her in 2008. Zoe went with us, as did my mother-in-law, who, at 75 years of age, had never been out of the country.

In the five years since we'd gotten Zoe, China had changed radically. Dull, gray Mao uniforms had been traded in for Western styles. Gone were many of the bicycles, replaced by exhaust-belching cars that clogged every artery through Beijing. The air was so polluted that the buildings hardly looked solid. It reminded me of the air in New York after the attack on the World Trade Center.

The country had turned into a nation of capitalists. Everywhere we went, someone tried to sell us something. At one restaurant, Marie complimented our server on the pretty dishes. He offered to sell her some, and she bought them.

Zoe had a hard time adjusting to the idea of China. We'd tried to explain it to her, but she didn't get it. As we walked through the Forbidden City, she looked around in fascination.

"Why are all the people Chinese?" she asked.

She didn't understand that China was a country, not a U.S. city.

When it was time to pick up Lian, our guide took us to an office building instead of a hotel. Two government officials waited in the room with us. We were the only family there to get a child. A car pulled up out front, and two nannies, one of which was albino and mute, got out. She carried Lian in and handed her over to Marie. The transaction felt cold and indifferent. The nannies swooped in and were gone in less than a minute. When they left, the government officials took over, flipping papers and pointing to where we were to sign. Lian screamed the whole time. Like Zoe, she was much thinner than her pictures had indicated. *What was going on with these children?* I wondered.

We soon found out why Lian had to be carried in. She could barely walk. Her knees didn't bend. Her gait closely resembled that of Frankenstein's monster. It seemed she'd never been given exercise to strengthen her leg muscles.

Zoe had expected a plump, energetic little sister. This was not the playmate she'd imagined. She didn't try to hide her disappointment.

Our guide delivered us back to our hotel and then disappeared for three days. Without a car or an interpreter, we were limited in our ability to move around the city. At meal times, I brought food back to the hotel room, but Lian wouldn't eat. Finally, I went to the dining room and asked them to prepare congee, a thin mixture of rice and milk or water often given to babies in China. She liked that.

Zoe didn't warm up to her new sister until one morning when the two were playing with Cheerios. Lian hadn't so much as cracked a smile in the two days she'd been with us, but as she and Zoe played, she giggled. What a beautiful sound that was! Zoe looked around at us in surprise.

"She laughed! Mommy, Daddy, did you hear? She laughed!"

"She sure did," I said. "She likes you. You're magic, Zoe."

Our guide returned in time to get us to the airport for the flight home.

Through her early years with us, Lian faced some challenges. In addition to her walking difficulties, she didn't speak at first. Of course, she didn't know English, so that accounted for part of her hesitancy, but not all. She made no attempt to speak in either language. Regular physical and speech therapy brought her up to speed on both counts.

Another situation that concerned us was that she wouldn't let us hug her. She refused demonstrations of affection. She'd accept our touching her during bathing and dressing, but she'd shove us away if we attempted to express our love with a hug. Then, one day, after Lian had been with us for two months, Marie stood her on her changing table to finish dressing her. Suddenly, Lian came toward her. At first, Marie thought Lian had lost her balance, falling forward, but she soon realized that was not the case. Lian was giving her a hug around the neck.

Zoe had her own set of troubles. While she had wanted a little sister, she hadn't counted on our having to divert to this newcomer some of the attention that had been solely hers. It took time and professional counseling to resolve those issues.

Lian overcame her challenges. To hear her years later, one would never suspect an early speech problem. She got to be a chatterbox. And a tomboy. Today, she loves to play baseball, and she's a die-hard Yankees fan. That's my fault. I set her in front of the TV when Derek Jeter hit his 300th homerun, and she's never been the same. Every year, we go to a couple of home games together.

꙳꙳꙳

"I'm going back to China on a mission. Which one of you wants to come along?" Our friend Anthony looked from Marie to me and back to her. "Marie? You're a doctor — a pediatrician. We sure could use you on the team."

Anthony was a nurse, and America World Adoption Association had asked him to lead a volunteer team to visit an orphanage. He also had adopted children from China.

Marie shook her head. "I know it would be great, but I really can't. China, with its polluted air, isn't a good place for someone like me, who has trouble breathing even clean air sometimes. I just can't."

"But I can," I said. They both looked at me. "Hey, sure, our girls are from China, but I never saw the inside of an orphanage there. I've kind of wanted to go back but never thought I would. I'm not a doctor. Or a nurse. But I'd love to go. Do you accept lawyers?"

Anthony laughed. "Well, not normally, but I think we could make an exception in your case."

"Everyone's a comedian. Seriously, though, I don't want to jump recklessly into something this important. Can I have some time to pray about it?"

"Yes, of course. You should do that. I'll get back with you in a few days."

I was on the plane when it left for China in October 2014, and I was in for a big shock.

ฝฝฝ

I grew up Roman Catholic. My family currently attends a huge Catholic church that holds multiple services each Sunday. I'm an introvert, so it isn't easy for me to mingle with people. Most of the congregants I'm familiar with are parents whose children attend Catholic school with my daughters. I go to church and observe the sacraments, but I don't feel a sense of community there. My family sits all alone in the crowd.

I live in the Greater New York area. I travel to and from work every day on crowded trains and subways where everyone avoids eye contact and conversation with strangers. Again, I stand — or, if I'm lucky, sit — shoulder to shoulder with people I don't know. Yet, I'm alone.

That autumn of 2014, I found myself in the company of 18 very different people. They were Christians. All of them. Followers of Jesus Christ. And they talked about it. Openly. With one another. And to anyone else who would listen, for that matter. To me!

Sometimes their openness about their faith made me a little nervous. No one else I knew did that. Well, except for Anthony. I knew him from church, specifically from the school. We'd connected because we both had daughters from China. Several members of this team had been on other missions together, so their community bond was strong.

I had no idea what to expect at the orphanage. I assumed there would be a mix of children — boys, girls, some healthy, some with special needs — but I was wrong. They *all* had disabilities of some kind.

Most common were the children with cleft palates, bright boys and girls with broken faces and amazing smiles. If only they could get the surgery needed to repair the palates. Or if only people with the resources to help would adopt them.

Some children had cerebral palsy, a disorder that can cause varying degrees of disability, from mild to severe. Others had hydrocephalus — water on the brain. They all appeared to be well cared for by the nannies, who worked hard to keep them and their surroundings clean.

When we arrived each day, the children greeted us with eager smiles. That amazed me. How could they be so happy? What did they have to smile about?

One boy caught my attention early on. He was 14 years old but small and frail. His arms and legs were very dark due to a lack of circulation. They appeared to be dead. But the boy, who was alert to his surroundings, had an easy smile. If you gave him a friendly touch on the arm, his smile broadened.

While most of the children were true orphans with no connection to their parents, some of the older boys had been brought to the orphanage by parents who wanted to keep them but could not provide for their special needs. Four boys who shared that common history had banded together as brothers, helping each other when playing games, enjoying playground equipment and eating. Each had figured out how best to help the others.

When we returned from that first mission trip, Anthony asked what I thought of the experience.

"It took some getting used to at first, but I loved it. The kids are amazing," I said.

Anthony chuckled. "Yes, the kids are that. So, can we plan on your being on the team next October?"

"If God wills it, absolutely!"

On that first trip, I realized that I'd spent too much time being mad at God. In China, I felt like he'd ripped the root of anger from my heart and planted in its place seeds of compassion and love for a hurting, broken world. I felt like God had given me new eyes to see what needed to be done — yes, internationally, but also around the corner from my house, across the street from my office and next door to my church.

I realized that not everyone could pack up and take off for the other side of the planet, but I also learned about many other ways to make a difference. Mission trips cost money. International travel is expensive. Some can foot their own bills, while others scurry to garner support. Many people who couldn't go themselves contributed money to help those who did go.

We cannot earn our way to heaven with good works, but they sure make life here on earth a better place. I could hardly wait to head back to China.

But it almost didn't happen for me.

❧❧❧

Shortly before Christmas 2014, just two months after returning from China, a stranger attacked me at the mall, throwing me to the pavement and beating me. I sustained a broken left knee. The orthopedic surgeon reconstructed my knee with six screws, bone grafting and a plate. I used crutches for three months. After that, I underwent physical therapy. The driving thought that motivated me and kept me on task with my physical therapy was that I had to get better so I could return to my kids in China. Their faces were ever before me. *Do it for the kids,* I told myself. *Push through the pain for God and the kids.*

❧❧❧

We will be your hands healing …
your feet walking into a broken world.
We will be your love!
[from "Won't You Be My Love" by MercyMe]

As great as the first mission trip was, the second trip was even better, perhaps because I was more at ease. I knew team members from the previous trip, and I knew what to expect. I also knew what was expected of me as my role expanded.

As a mission team, we had one main goal: to be the hands, feet and love of Jesus to the children. In addition, we gathered information about the children who were eligible for adoption. My role included taking more photographs of the children, both formal profile shots and candid pictures. I also helped organize videos of the children at play, capturing for potential adoptive parents an idea of each child's personality and abilities.

Anthony and the other team leader, Charlotte, divided us into four smaller teams that rotated among the four main areas of the orphanage: two infant rooms and two rooms with older children. One of the latter housed children so severely disabled that they likely would not be adopted — a fact that grieved us all.

We spent nine hours a day at the orphanage, communicating with the children through interpreters, playing with them, praying for them and leading various crafts and activities. They reveled in the attention. One member of our team, Aria, played her guitar and sang to them. They loved the music. If she played a fast song, those who could dance around did so. Others simply swayed or clapped to the rhythm.

Aria had a special love for the younger children — the toddlers and babies.

"They have no one to sing them to sleep with lullabies," she said, so she wrote a lullaby especially for them.

Each team member had someone he or she connected with, and many desired to adopt their special child. I also wanted to, but I didn't think it would be possible.

Everyone loved Jill. She was a little girl of toddler age, but she couldn't be up and around because she had hydrocephalus. Hers had been diagnosed early on, so her head wasn't much larger than normal, just large enough that she needed support. She had a shunt to keep fluid from accumulating.

Jill had a sweet personality that won our hearts. Once she was propped up, she laughed and played with the other children. While we were there, she had not been approved for adoption, but two months after we returned stateside, I was notified that her paperwork had come through, making her a candidate for adoption. Someone from the home office of America World Adoption Association asked if I could write up a report about her.

I didn't hesitate. "Absolutely." I also began praying that she'd get adopted.

That sense of community I'd experienced on my first mission trip deepened on the second one. At the end of each day, all 20 members of the team crowded into one of our hotel rooms for worship time. Together, we prayed for the children and staff of the orphanage, as well as for one another. We shared stories about our day. I played Aria's guitar and led the others in singing hymns and worship choruses such as "Amazing Grace," "Christ Is Enough," "How Deep the Father's Love" and "Lord, I Need You." Charlotte presented a devotional each time we gathered, and sometimes people would tell about something that had blessed them.

I believe that God used those times together to teach me the value and power of community. His community. I had read in the Bible about the body of Christ, but I hadn't really understood it until I became part of the mission team. We *were* one body, part of the greater body of Christ. No one part was more important than another. We all had a purpose.

Through the experience of both trips, I also saw how God changed my worldview completely. I realized that when he shows us the people of the world as he sees them, and sees us, through the eyes of love, there is no room for personal pride.

On the last day before we left for home, we threw a huge party at the orphanage — one big supersized birthday party for all the kids. We had a blast laughing, singing, dancing, playing games, eating cake and laughing some more. Then we sang "Happy Birthday" twice: once in English, and once in Chinese.

We had to go out laughing, lest we cry for sorrow of having to leave the children we loved so much. But they knew by then that many of us would return. Hopefully, "Uncle Joel" (as some of the kids called me) will be in that number another October.

࿐࿐࿐

I am not an old man. Yet, I have known much trauma, much sorrow. I witnessed firsthand the tragedy of the 9/11 terrorist attacks. I suffered a brutal physical assault by a hate-consumed stranger and endured the ensuing surgery, disability and painful therapy necessary to regain the use of my knee. After returning from the second trip, a close

CRADLES IN Q CITY

friend gave birth prematurely to a beautiful baby boy who lived less than a week. I've walked with my dear Marie through her life-threatening breathing problems, the result of her own premature birth. I've spent long hours in prayer for my beloved daughters, Zoe and Lian.

Through all that, I've come to realize God is not random. Everything we experience is for a purpose.

Having known my own suffering, I can show compassion toward a smiling boy who can hardly move because his limbs are dead.

I can laugh with a little girl whose head needs support so she can play ball with me.

When I'm helping a boy whose legs are in braces climb up the ladder of a slide, I understand, because I've been disabled, too.

I have an all-consuming passion to serve Jesus Christ by serving others who need to experience his love. As Jesus says in Matthew 25:40, "Truly I tell you, whatever you did for one of the least of these brothers and sisters of mine, you did for me."

"Just as a body, though one, has many parts, but all its
many parts form one body, so it is with Christ …
If one part suffers, every part suffers with it;
if one part is honored, every part rejoices with it."
(1 Corinthians 12:12, 12:26 NIV)

AN INCREDIBLE GIFT
The Story of Anthony
Written by Lisa Bradshaw

My wife, Kayla, and I decided to adopt a child from China. As we prepared to share our plans with friends and family members, I found myself feeling nervous about telling my father. He came from Italy, and he had a strong pride in our Italian heritage. I couldn't predict his reaction to our announcement.

My mom responded as I anticipated she would — with great excitement about meeting her first grandchild.

"Oh, Anthony! I'm so happy for you!" Mom exclaimed as she hugged my neck and reached for Kayla. She cried tears of joy. "Kayla! A baby! So wonderful!"

Mom knew we'd wanted to conceive but had faced infertility issues. Both Kayla and I took comfort in her enthusiasm and acceptance when we announced our big news.

After telling Mom, I walked toward the garage of my parents' home and found Dad working on a new project.

"Hey, Pops."

"Hey."

"How's it going?"

"Good. Good."

"So, I wanted to let you know Kayla and I have made a big decision."

"Yeah, what's that?"

"We've decided to adopt a little girl from China."

He must've sensed my reluctance to share our news with him for fear of his reaction. He stopped working and turned toward me, looking me straight in the eyes.

"Son, a child is a child, no matter where the child comes from."

కాలాంత

At age 24, I contracted Hodgkin's disease. The shock and dismay overwhelmed my family and me. When I learned about the risks of treatment, I felt an added dimension of fear.

Even if I survive, I may never be able to have children.

But I recognized that I could face only one fear at a time. First, I had to face cancer. Later down the road, I could deal with the effects of my treatment.

Chemotherapy wreaked havoc on my body, caused my hair to fall out and left me almost unrecognizable.

After several months of treatment, tests showed no remaining cancer.

My outlook on life changed considerably. Before having cancer, I had little direction in my life. Besides knowing that I wanted to marry my best friend, Kayla, I didn't know what I wanted or how I would provide for a family one day. But after going through my diagnosis and treatment, my ideas about a chosen career path became clear to me.

After receiving care from wonderful nurses, I felt eager to help other patients in the same way. I knew the comfort that a good nurse offered and the frustration caused by those with less competence or compassion.

I wanted to be the bright side of someone's medical experience. Becoming a nurse felt like the most rewarding way to transform my experience with cancer.

Kayla stood by me the entire time. Even after realizing that the chemotherapy might leave me infertile, she still saw her future with me.

We married eight days after my last treatment. She also supported my decision to enroll in nursing school, encouraging me throughout my studies and celebrating with me when I graduated five years later.

We both worked hard in our careers, we made a good living and we tried for a long time for Kayla to become pregnant.

Each month that passed with a failed pregnancy test left us feeling more and more hopeless about the possibility that we might ever have children.

Years passed, but we kept trying. And we felt disappointment every time Kayla had to break the news to me that she wasn't pregnant. Sometimes, I wondered if she'd regretted deciding to marry me.

"What if we adopt a baby from China?" Kayla asked me one evening, nine years after we'd started trying to conceive.

"Adopt?" I asked. "Are you sure that's something you want to do?"

"I think it's a good idea," she said. "It's probably time to start thinking about adopting, and we've both heard about children in need of adoption in China."

Neither of us knew anything about the actual process for adopting a child from China, but we'd certainly heard of people who'd successfully completed international adoptions.

Kayla and I prayed together and separately about it, and we both ultimately felt like God was leading us to pursue adoption.

Once we made the decision, we both dove into researching the process and learning which agency had the best reputation and the most success for completed adoptions. We decided on America World Adoption Association, a Christian adoption agency, and its healthy-child program, which meant that we would adopt a healthy child without any known medical needs. Kayla and I both wanted to use the assistance and guidance of a Christian agency because we felt strongly that adoption should be facilitated by people who see their work as a calling from God rather than a business transaction.

Early in the process, we felt overwhelmed when we received the application forms and a list of documents required from us. The checklist included copies of our birth certificates, our marriage license, proof of residency for places we'd lived and our fingerprints. The documents seemed like logical and routine paperwork for adopting a child, but locating and getting the documents verified and certified required several steps and felt daunting. But we never considered giving up our newfound dream to adopt a child from China — no matter how long it took or how much paperwork it involved.

"I think that's it," I told Kayla as I handed her the last of the documents, and she checked each one off the list.

She smiled. "That's it."

❧❧❧

Within a year of applying for adoption, Kayla and I stepped off a plane in China to meet our daughter. The agency informed us ahead of time that upon arrival, we'd spend a couple of days visiting the sights and getting acquainted with the local culture. We'd meet our daughter a few days later. We arrived late on a Friday and visited the Great Wall of China the next day.

"Did you ever think, in all your life, you and I would be standing at the Great Wall of China?" I asked Kayla.

"No, never." She and I laughed.

We enjoyed our initial days in China, but we couldn't wait to meet our daughter. We'd been told the schedule: On Monday morning, we'd be taken by car to the province of our baby's orphanage. We'd stay in the area about a week as we bonded with our child before returning home to the United States.

The agency did a good job of preparing us for the logistics of our stay, but nothing could prepare us for the moment we saw our daughter for the first time and held her in our arms.

CRADLES IN Q CITY

"Robertson," someone called out, holding a baby.

The Robertsons approached their adoptive baby with excitement.

"Reynolds," another called out a few minutes later.

One by one, nannies and babies entered a large room at the local social welfare institute. We watched as each embarked upon the new adventure of becoming a family.

"Abbatelli," we finally heard someone say.

"That's us," I said, holding Kayla's hand. I immediately recognized our daughter from the photos we'd received.

The nanny placed our daughter, Li Li, in my wife's arms, and the two of us immediately cried as we hugged her. Li Li had just turned 1 year old and seemed rather unfazed by our presence and everything else happening in the room.

"She's beautiful," Kayla cried.

"And look how calm she is with us," I observed. "We've waited for you so long," I said to Li Li. For almost 10 years of marriage, we had longed for a child. All that time, we trusted that God would build us a family, even if it wasn't the way we'd expected. We cried, other parents cried, babies cried and siblings jumped up and down with excitement, but Li Li just looked around the room and at us. She observed everything and took it all in.

I hadn't known what to expect from the experience of visiting a foreign country and having a stranger place a baby — whom I'd never met but would be my child — in our arms. As Kayla and I stood in the crowded room holding Li Li, I felt the enormity of the gift we'd been given. I considered every prayer we'd said, every paper we'd filled out and every document we'd tracked down. All of it culminated in that moment. Instantly, just like when a father in the delivery room cuts the umbilical cord and holds his newborn child for the first time, I became Li Li's father.

❧❧❧

Kayla and I spent the next several days in and out of our hotel room with Li Li. We got to know her and took care of her. She remained quiet and observant. She didn't cry, but eventually she smiled and laughed as we played with her each day. Still, nothing seemed to faze her, and she remained content in our company.

We arrived home after a long two weeks in China, to the excitement of our family, friends and people at church, who were all anxious to meet Li Li. Everyone expressed such joy and showed so much love to the three of us. My mom and dad both adored Li Li and relished their roles as her grandparents. In time, we settled into our new family routine. I went back to work, and Kayla left her full-time job to stay at home with our daughter.

We'd made the decision to adopt again before even leaving China with Li Li, but the policy at the time required us to wait six months to a year before submitting a new application. Meanwhile, we continued bonding with Li Li and enjoying our new life as a family.

Unfortunately, things changed in China in just a short

period of time. The regulations became stricter shortly after we adopted Li Li.

The first hurdle we faced came when we filled out the initial health questionnaire about our medical history. Previously, my cancer history hadn't been a factor, but the second time, it eliminated us completely from the option to adopt through the healthy-child program.

"Maybe God intends for us to adopt only one child from China," I said, feeling frustrated that cancer had again hindered our ability to bring a child into our lives. "We waited a year for Li Li, and now with all the changes in policies, the wait for a healthy child is two and a half years. And that's if we can even adopt a healthy child, given my medical history."

"There's got to be another option," Kayla tried to encourage me. "We'll find a way."

With Kayla also determined to adopt again and certainly not blaming my medical history — or me — for this hiccup in the process, we continued forward and decided to adopt through the special-needs program of AWAA. This meant that we agreed to adopt a child with special needs, knowing we'd learn about the specific needs of the child before making a commitment.

"It's a bit bizarre that we have to fill out a checklist of medical needs that we are willing to consider," Kayla said.

We spent time discussing all the possibilities and prayed about how we should answer the pressing items on the questionnaire. The form gave the option to check "yes," "no" or "possibly" for various health conditions.

"Let's just not say 'no' to anything," I suggested after we'd prayed about it for a few days. "Let's say 'yes' to everything except heart defects. Let's answer 'possibly' to that option." As a nurse, I knew the challenges faced in children with heart defects, so I felt it might be best to avoid that possibility.

"And if a child with a heart defect is offered to us, we'll decide then," Kayla added.

We agreed and filled out the paperwork accordingly.

Our relatives, friends and people at church asked us almost every week if we'd heard anything.

"It'll be at least a year from now before we hear," Kayla and I would answer.

We didn't expect to hear anything back from the agency about a potential child for our family for quite a while. We tried not to let the wait interfere with our everyday lives, but we both wondered about our next child. We couldn't wait to bring another baby home.

Within just five months of joining the special-needs program to adopt a second child from China, Kayla received a call about a baby becoming available for adoption.

"I'm looking at a picture of a little girl with white skin, white hair and beautiful blue eyes," Kayla said when calling me at work with the news. "We have 72 hours to decide. Do you want to wait until you come home and see the picture before we decide?"

"Nope, that's our daughter," I answered. "I don't need to see the picture. That's our daughter."

Kayla and I felt strongly about relying on God to help build our family. We believed that if a particular child became available to us, then we would embrace the opportunity to become her parents.

Later, Kayla told me that she knew our next child would have albinism.

"How did you know?" I asked her.

"I'm not sure. I just knew."

ৡৡৡ

Our next hurdle during our second adoption had nothing to do with policy and more to do with finances. When we'd started the process to adopt Li Li, both of us were working full time, and we'd had money in savings. This time, we approached adoption while living on one income and having little savings. We'd scheduled our trip to China, but we still needed several thousand dollars to finalize adoption fees and travel. We'd applied for a grant through Show Hope, an organization that helps fund adoptions and provides life-giving care in some areas of China. In order to aid our adoption fundraising, we held a bake sale at church and raised $2,700. We never knew we would be able to raise so much through baked goods, but our church family was generous. We also found out that we'd received a $4,000 grant from Show Hope. These two efforts enabled us to raise exactly the amount we needed. We could go to China.

Our family of three flew to China to meet Li Li's new

sister and our new daughter. Just like the first time, we gathered in a large room, where nannies brought children to the new parents adopting them. As the nanny placed our 22-month-old daughter, Mai, in Kayla's arms, we felt overjoyed to have added another daughter to our family. Li Li took to Mai immediately.

When we returned home, we took several steps to help Mai adjust to our new home. We immediately sought help with early intervention in occupational, speech and physical therapy and started her in visual therapy. The albinism had left her legally blind. None of the physical hurdles we helped Mai face challenged us as much as the emotional toll her behavior took on us.

"Mai seems most content just sitting on the floor rocking herself and bumping her head against the wall as stimulation," Kayla told me.

"I know. We always intervene when we see her do it, but as soon as she finds herself alone in a room, she does it again," I added.

Mai also had repetitive behaviors when playing with a toy, like putting a rubber duck on her bottom lip and opening and closing her mouth. She acted as if she didn't know what to do with toys or how to receive our attention when we tried interacting with her with the toy in her hand. We'd show her a different way to handle the toy, and she'd go right back to the repetitive behavior. In my profession as a nurse, I had learned the characteristics of neglected children. I felt certain Mai had been severely neglected during her time at the orphanage. We didn't blame the nannies or the orphanage. The child-to-nanny ratio is often 10 to one, and they stay quite busy taking care of the children's daily physical needs.

Despite these initial challenges, Mai quickly became an affectionate child. She always shared a smile with strangers. As we had done with Li Li, we taught her to pray and told her about God's love.

About two years after we brought Mai home, we started thinking about adopting a third child. Once we decided to move forward with adopting again, we found out that the regulations in China had become even stricter than they had been when we'd adopted Mai. This time, my medical history excluded us from any opportunity of adopting through the healthy or waiting child programs. As an alternative, the agency introduced us to the special focus program. The special focus program allowed the parents to request an exception to adopt a waiting child if the child's file was designated as "special focus by China."

"Do you have a preference of age?" Kayla asked me. Children in China couldn't be adopted after age 14.

"Age doesn't matter to me," I answered.

Again, Kayla and I put our trust in God to build our family. Within a short time, we chose a 12-year-old girl named Song. From the orphanage's description, she had some health issues, but they said she was a good worker who helped the nannies at the orphanage. The agency also told us that she didn't talk very much and kept to herself a lot. We'd experienced the same isolation behaviors with Mai when she first came home, but since she had quickly warmed up to us and everyone around her, we figured Song would likely do the same. The moment we chose Song, we considered her our daughter and didn't sway from our decision. We just wanted to gather all the information we could about Song to help us all prepare for bringing her home.

We flew to China as a family to adopt Song. Li Li and Mai couldn't wait to meet their older sister and bring her home. We felt excitement as well, and we embraced her with love and joy just as we had done with our other two daughters when meeting them for the first time in China. Each time we adopted a child, we called our day of meeting our "Family Day." We didn't rely on the adoption agency's signed paperwork 24 hours later to dictate when we became a family. We celebrated from the moment we held each child in our arms.

Right away, we noticed that Song had a disconnected stare and didn't share our emotions. When we met our other daughters, Li Li had been quiet and observant, and Mai had been a busy toddler. But Song seemed to look through us, never making a connection through eye contact or responding to our touch when we hugged her or put a hand on her shoulder. On our flight home from China, Song showed no response to the plane shaking or lifting off the ground, even though she'd never flown before. When we arrived home and Li Li and Mai tried playing with Song, she showed no response. We realized that Song might not know how to play. She seemed to prefer not to play at all.

Song's paperwork from the orphanage hadn't noted any cognitive delays or specific health issues, but we soon realized that her inability to make eye contact was not merely a social and emotional hurdle, but an indication of a vision problem. We took her to several doctors in hopes of understanding how we could educate her and help her adjust. Song's health issues and other circumstances had prevented her from going to school when she lived in the orphanage. In China, education isn't free, so not everyone is eligible to receive an education — particularly an orphan child with Song's medical circumstances.

"I wonder if we did the right thing," I confided in Barbara, a family friend. "I love her just as much as I love our other daughters, but I wonder if we did what's best for Song. Would she have been better off staying in the orphanage? At least there she would have been able to remain in the orphanage when she turned 14 and become a nanny, living and doing all she'd ever known."

"But she never would have known the love of family," Barbara replied.

My eyes welled up with tears at the thought of Song growing into an old woman and never receiving the love of a family. Barbara's words marked a turning point. I took them as a gift and a lesson from God to no longer question our decision to adopt Song. We said from the beginning that we'd put our faith in God to build our family, so I trusted that God had chosen Song for us. If we hadn't adopted her when we did, in just two short years she wouldn't have had the option to be adopted. We may have been her last opportunity to know the love of a family. In that brief yet profound exchange with Barbara, I felt peace and acceptance about the family I believe God had provided for us.

᭡᭡᭡

"I feel like God is calling us to be more involved in orphan care," I said to Kayla one evening after putting the kids to bed.

"As if bringing the girls home to our family is just the beginning?" she asked.

"Exactly," I replied.

"I feel the same way," she agreed.

Within three years of adopting Song, I received an email from AWAA about the need for team leaders to help organize volunteer trips to orphanages in China. I replied to the email expressing my interest and soon began the application process.

Within the application, I explained our experience adopting three children from China. I shared our concerns about the signs of emotional neglect we had witnessed in Mai and the challenges Song faced because of her lack of education. I also noted the importance of receiving an accurate assessment of the children when adopting, especially in Song's case. We wouldn't have changed our minds about adopting her, but we feel we could have better prepared for her arrival if we had known the details of her health issues before bringing her home.

Even so, Song had grown to welcome our love and become a willing participant in our family life. We encouraged others not to fear the prospect of adopting older children.

Within a year of receiving the initial email from AWAA, I went on my first volunteer trip. I didn't get to visit one of the orphanages our daughters came from, but I knew many orphanages faced the same challenges.

During the trip to Q City's orphanage, the American team members played with the children and spent time educating the nannies about ways to stimulate the children's growth and development while taking care of their physical needs — like talking with them while changing their diapers and gently rubbing their heads.

We knew the nannies worked hard every day, so we didn't try adding to their jobs. We just tried giving them the tools to interact with the children more often on an emotional level.

Many of the nannies had grown up in orphanages, so the things we suggested didn't come naturally to them, but they remained open and began implementing our ideas right away.

I came home from that trip with a much better understanding of the daily happenings in the orphanages. I couldn't wait to return, and I quickly started planning to participate in the next volunteer trip.

ৡৡৡ

AN INCREDIBLE GIFT

"Welcome," the director said when greeting us the following year. "Please, come inside." We returned to the same orphanage the second time and were welcomed like old friends. As I interacted with the director, I gained a better understanding of how vital it was for men to participate in volunteer trips. Most who went on such trips were women, and the addition of male participants seemed to help build relationships with the director and bridge the gap between identifying needs and taking action to meet those needs.

Our second volunteer trip still involved helping and educating the nannies and playing with the children, but it focused more on identifying medical needs that might otherwise have gone undetected and, if not addressed, could compromise the children's chances of survival. Then we helped clarify the assessments that the orphanage would later provide to potential adoptive parents.

"These two have a diagnosis of spina bifida," a doctor traveling with us observed while examining the children.

"What else does it say?" I asked.

"Nothing else. Just spina bifida," he answered. "These are two high-functioning children with very mild forms of the disease, yet none of this is noted in their files."

A diagnosis of spina bifida can refer to a great range of conditions, and these children had the mildest form of the disease. Yet anyone who might have wanted to adopt them wouldn't have known that, because the file didn't specify the level of spina bifida. Our new assessments updated the files and provided potential adoptive parents with more

accurate and encouraging information about the children's needs and potential. Providing more accurate medical information would likely improve each child's chance of being adopted.

Each time I observed the children in the orphanage, I couldn't help but think about Li Li, Mai and Song. For every child who'd been adopted, more children remained without parents and opportunities to be part of a family. When I considered the sequence of events and decisions that led Kayla and me to adopt and, later, to work to improve the circumstances for other orphans, I wondered if any of this would have happened had I not been diagnosed with cancer and become infertile.

If I had the ability to father children, would we have considered adoption from China? Would we each be returning to orphanages yearly to help improve the quality of life for the children still waiting for adoption?

Contemplating these things always brings me to gratitude for all I gained from the experience of cancer. I survived it. Nothing bad came from it. Kayla and I tried for nine years to get pregnant, but it didn't tear us apart. It made us stronger. It set us in the direction of our daughters and all the other children still waiting for a family. I firmly believe that nothing we've endured or accomplished could have been possible without God in the center of it.

As I became part of the work of Love Without Boundaries, I felt further blessed to be part of something so organized and succinct in its mission. LWB is an orphan-care agency founded by mothers who adopted children from China. It provides services based on the needs of various orphanages. Some orphanages had nutritional needs for babies with cleft lip, so LWB provided special bottles and nutritional supplements for feeding those children. If a child had a medical defect, Love Without Boundaries helped facilitate a transport for the child to a hospital for surgery. They also helped place the child in a "healing home" with a ratio of two to four children to one nanny so the children could recover in a hands-on environment before returning to the orphanage.

After our first trip, we raised funds beyond our needed budget, so in partnership with America World Adoption, we donated a portion of the additional funds to Love Without Boundaries. They used the money to implement a school in the orphanage and had it fully functioning within three months. When we returned the following year, we saw the results of our donation in full use. In addition to starting the school, the orphanage also had enough funds to provide additional feeding options for the children with cleft lips.

Our first daughter, Li Li, came home to us healthy and easily adjusted to life in a loving and happy home. Our second daughter, Mai, struggled at first to bond because of emotional and tactile neglect. Our third daughter, Song, lived 12 years without an education or the comprehensive therapy she needed for development. Each of our daughter's experiences made Kayla and me more aware of the needs of the children in China and in orphanages around the world. The volunteer trips showed me that even small efforts can change the world's orphan crisis.

Providing information and training for the nannies, conducting medical assessments, taking pictures and videos, and raising money for surgeries and needed supplies are just a few examples of how one team influenced one orphanage in Q City and helped children find forever families.

When I look at my daughters and the challenges they've faced and overcome, it pushes me to keep visiting orphanages and bringing hope and support to the children, nannies and leaders of these orphanages. I believe that God's plan for Kayla, our family and me has been unfolding for a long time. Ever since the first time we shared the news of adoption with our families, we have all been blessed by the wonderful girls we brought home to make part of our family. I watch my father's face light up when he sees and plays with his granddaughters, and I wonder how I could have ever doubted his approval.

We put our trust in God to help us build our family, and we continue to place our trust in him to help bring us to the aid of the children still waiting for a home. The cancer diagnosis I survived helped bring us here, leaving me with a better understanding of how God can take a tragedy and turn it into an incredible gift.

A MILLION LITTLE MIRACLES
The Story of Charlotte
Written by Amy Green

"In the event of a water landing, your seat cushion can be used as a flotation device."

The flight attendant smiled as she spoke. I imagined she must be pretty sick of making the safety speech, so I tried to pay attention.

I was flying home from China for the third summer in a row. While I couldn't wait to kiss my husband, I never enjoyed leaving China. This flight home felt even more impossible, because now I knew May.

I closed my eyes and began to pray, hoping that my prayers might gradually shift into sleep that would last most of the long flight.

God, thank you for being with me while I taught English this summer. Help me remember how desperately I needed you and how quickly you answered my prayers. I don't want to get back home and forget what it feels like to have a living, active God guiding me through every day, just because I have classes to plan, dishes to wash and a husband to love.

Oh, and God, please be close to May. Love her and be her family. I can't imagine growing up in an orphanage without a family, but she is so beautiful and sweet. I don't understand why no one ever adopted her. God, how can girls like May not know what it is like to have a family? Help me remember May for the rest of my life. Please make a way for my husband and me to adopt a sweet baby girl from China someday. When I tell Oliver about May, help him understand somehow. Oh, Jesus, I know adoption feels too big and overwhelming and there are so many kids who need homes, but you gave me one beautiful face to remember. Please give everyone who wants to help and doesn't know how a face to identify with. A face like May's.

I spent the flight sleeping in spurts, crying at beautiful memories of China from that year and the past two trips, and fighting the stress that started to creep in as I thought of all the obligations that waited for me at home.

When I finally walked off the last airplane, my husband waited with flowers. I ran up to him, tears streaming down my face, hugged him tightly and kissed him.

"I missed you so much, Oliver."

"I missed you, too."

"Have you been here long?"

"Not too long. I wanted to see your plane land."

I slipped my hand into Oliver's and felt the butterflies I first felt as a teenager. I married him right after high school, and six years later, he was still my best friend. Taking these trips to China every summer to teach English was one of the only experiences I didn't share with him. I tried to describe everything for him, but the words I spoke never painted a full enough picture.

"I have so much I want to tell you, and oh, this time I went to an orphanage. I met all these beautiful children, and there was this girl, May. She was probably 10 or 11, and I just fell in love with her. I wanted to bring her home. It broke my heart to leave her there."

"I'm so sorry," Oliver said.

"I just don't even understand why there are orphans. How can anyone meet a child like May and not just say, 'Yes! Of course you can be my child.' It's kind of like I always knew that God told us to love and take care of orphans in their distress, but May made that real for me, and I feel like we have to adopt a baby from China someday."

"I agree."

"Really, Oliver?"

"Sure, honey. Let's have a few babies and then adopt a baby."

"I would love that."

Part of me wondered if I really felt ready to be a mother. I didn't want to give up my trips to China. With college finished, there was no reason to put it off. I glanced out the airport window at the plane and wondered how many more trips I could fit in. We both wanted a big family, so we couldn't wait much longer to get started.

"Oh, Charlotte," Oliver said. "You look like you could fall over right here. Let's get you home."

❧❧❧

"Okay, just lie down here, and you'll have to scooch down a little. A little spotting can be normal during pregnancy, but let's just see what's going on, okay?"

I looked over at Oliver holding Nathaniel in his arms. I almost couldn't believe that just a year earlier, I was still just pregnant with Nathaniel — and here we were, with Nathaniel smiling and laughing and just starting to sit up on his own, and I was pregnant with this new sweet baby growing inside of me, making us a family of four.

I thought of the full life we were already living. After I met May, I took one more trip to China. Then we decided to have a baby, and Nathaniel filled my heart in a way I never expected. We wanted four children before we adopted a daughter from China, but we weren't planning to have a second baby so quickly.

A wrinkle formed on the forehead of the ultrasound technician. I noticed she hadn't said anything for a while. I didn't want to break her concentration, but something felt wrong. Even two weeks earlier, when she said the baby measured small, something felt off. I tried to ignore my fears, but they seemed to spring to life on the face of this woman staring at the monitor.

She stopped moving the Doppler and turned the screen toward us.

"I can see the baby here, but unfortunately, there is no heartbeat. I'm so sorry."

I began to cry.

God, don't let this be true. Don't let it be true. Oh, God, please.

I knew, even as I prayed, that my baby was gone.

I looked up at Oliver, wiping away my tears that just kept coming. He put Nathaniel in my arms and held both of us as I wept. Nathaniel gurgled and smiled, not a big brother anymore, but still so perfect. Even if we never had another baby, at least we had Nathaniel.

The following days passed in a blur. Oliver made the phone calls to our friends and family, telling them what we hadn't told anyone yet: that I was pregnant. And what we wished we never had to tell anyone ever: that our baby had died.

꙳꙳꙳

My life didn't feel like my own. I knew miscarriages were common, but somehow I never understood how tragic it really felt for the parents. Lingering hope kept the grief fresh.

Our doctor told us we could wait and see if my body would take care of things on its own, or we could have a D&E. I still felt pregnant every day, and I couldn't imagine spending any more time waiting for something so terrible, so we agreed to have the D&E.

I looked over at Oliver as he drove me to the appointment. "I hate this so much!"

"I know." Oliver never said very much, but he usually found the words I needed when I needed them.

"I just keep hoping there will be some miracle, like I'll feel a kick and tell the doctors to do another ultrasound."

"That's why they tested the hormones in your blood, too. They wanted to be sure, and they are sure."

"I just wish we could go back to a few weeks ago when everything was still okay."

"Me, too."

I woke up from the procedure feeling groggy and sad. Oliver had tissues ready. He smiled sweetly at me and ran his hand through my hair.

"Tomorrow is Valentine's Day," I said.

"I know, Charlotte. The house is so full of flowers for you from all of our friends. It will feel like we live inside of a Valentine's card."

I shook my head. "That means today is the 13th, and this baby was due on the 13th of September, so we had seven months to go. In seven months, we were supposed to walk out of this hospital with a baby in our arms."

"We know that God is in control of our lives and our baby is in heaven."

"Will you pray for this baby with me?" I asked.

"Of course."

"God, I know you love our baby even more than we do." I began to cry, choking on the words. Oliver continued the prayer, sharing my heart in his own words.

"Thank you, Jesus, for preparing a place for this baby," he prayed. "We know that we will join you and our baby one day, and until then, we continue to trust you with our lives and this sweet baby we never got to hold in our arms."

I continued. "Thank you, God, for my husband and

the way he covers me with his love and reassures me of your love. Comfort him, too, God, and help us be the parents you want us to be to Nathaniel even while we grieve. We pray these things together in the name of Jesus. Amen."

I took several tissues from the box and wiped away tears. The nurse came in to check my vitals. I noticed the date written on her clipboard.

"Honey," I said. "Today is Friday the 13th. Did you know that?"

"I guess I didn't really put it together," Oliver replied. "I mean, I knew it was the 13th and a Friday, but I guess it feels appropriate."

ﾎﾎﾎ

"I'm so hungry. When are your parents going to get here?" Oliver asked.

I shooed him away from the plate of deviled eggs on the counter. More than two of them had already disappeared.

"They should get here in just a few minutes, and then we can eat right away," I told him. "Want to help me get the table set?"

Oliver dutifully took plates out to the dining room, and I followed him with the glasses. As I reached across the table, my belly brushed up against the edge of the table. I constantly forgot to accommodate the growing bulge.

In about a month, I'll be able to start feeling this baby's movements, I thought. *The little kicks will help me remember I'm pregnant, and the poor little thing won't get bumped into so many counters.*

I heard a car pull up, so I opened the front door.

"Come out here. You have to see this rainbow."

My mother looked just over the roof of our house, genuinely thrilled.

I looked at Oliver. Now his dinner would be postponed by rainbow gazing. "I'm sure it's beautiful, Mom, but I don't want dinner to get cold."

"Oh, no. You have to come see it. It's spectacular. Grab your camera. You've never seen anything like this," she said.

Oliver brought me the camera, and we stepped outside.

Oh, wow, she's right, I thought. *This is amazing.*

A rainbow spread directly over our house, bright and full. I snapped photo after photo. I didn't know rainbows could look this close.

It's just so beautiful.

కావావ

My nesting instincts were kicking in. I wanted to get caught up on all the laundry before going into labor with our son Paul.

Our computer's screen saver scrolled through photos stored on the computer. The photos of the rainbow from the dinner with my parents several months earlier caught my eye.

I stopped in the middle of the living room with the laundry basket on my hip to look at the photos again. I set the laundry down and sat at the computer. I noticed the date in the corner of the rainbow photos: September 13, 2004.

Oh, God, the rainbow. You put it there just for me?

Tears spilled down my face. I felt a little guilty that the due date had come and gone without me noticing.

September 13 was the due date for our baby. You remembered even when I forgot. Oh, God, thank you. I know you are loving our baby and remembering our pain even as we heal.

࿇࿇࿇

"In just a few weeks, life is going to get pretty busy around here," I said.

"It sure is, baby, but you're so great at helping our boys and keeping up the house. Most women would have collapsed under all the stress of chasing after Nathaniel, Paul and Ben, even if they weren't eight months pregnant." Oliver smiled at me.

"I just like to keep things in order. Staying on top of everything actually helps me relax."

"Are you ready to have four boys?"

"Ready or not, here he comes, right?"

"Right."

CRADLES IN Q CITY

A little feeling of dread started to settle into my chest, so I took a moment for a silent prayer.

Oh, God. Thank you for caring about all the little details. You orchestrate things so perfectly, but please, God, don't let our son be born on February 13. I know the due date is that week, but I just can't bear the idea of Joseph being born on the anniversary of leaving the hospital without our baby. I want his birthday to be a happy day. Thank you for hearing my prayers, Jesus. Amen.

৵৵৵৵

Jesus heard our prayers. I offered up a prayer of thanksgiving.

He is so beautiful and just perfect. Thanks for Oliver's strength and support. I love you, God.

Joseph yawned a sleepy little yawn that seemed to take over his entire face. Oliver and I laughed.

"You did good, Charlotte," Oliver told me.

"Thanks. I love you."

"I love you, too."

I felt so tired, but I didn't want to sleep. With each of our babies, the precious first days together in the hospital flew by too quickly and blurred together. I knew this would be my last hospital stay with a newborn in my arms. I wanted to memorize Joseph's face, the feeling of the soft skin on his back, the way Oliver looked at me while I nursed our new son.

We had never let go of the idea of adopting a baby girl from China. Now we had the four children we had always talked about having before beginning the adoption process.

"It's so quiet here, Oliver. I'm not used to it. A night with just the three of us. Do you remember being here with Nathaniel? I couldn't wait to get home then. Now, it feels like a retreat. A little peaceful cocoon for us and baby Joseph. I almost wish we didn't have to go home tomorrow, but I miss the boys, and they are so excited to have their new baby brother at home."

"It's nice to go home on a Friday. We'll have the weekend to get our bearings."

His words set my thoughts in motion, and I began to cry so hard that I almost couldn't get my words out intelligibly.

"Oh, honey. Tomorrow is Friday, February 13. Just like the day we left the hospital five years ago. It is a Friday the 13th exactly five years later, but this time we will have Joseph in our arms as we walk out the doors."

"God is so good."

I knew Oliver was right; this timing felt like redemption.

"I almost can't believe it. We have four sons now, and life keeps marching forward, but God doesn't forget the baby we lost."

❧❧❧

They are so precious to God. These beautiful children — no one sees their value, but God does, and he says they are precious.

Face after face filled the screen as the presenter on the stage at church continued to talk about the sponsorship program to help take care of children in impoverished countries.

I turned to Oliver. "I can't help but think of May. Her face made orphans real for me. Maybe these faces are enough to change someone's heart at this concert. Do you know she is 19 or 20 now? An adult, making a life for herself."

"Wow, it's hard to believe it's been that long. Do you miss your trips to China?" Oliver asked.

"So much, but this season of life is beautiful, too — just busier. I'm sure I can go back someday."

An usher came to our aisle and handed a bucket to the person at the end of our row. As it passed from hand to hand, a few people reached in to take sponsorship packets. I grabbed a packet and handed the bucket to Oliver, who passed it on to the person on his left. I opened the packet and ripped out the sponsorship card. I started filling it out before I noticed that my husband had not said a word.

"You're not saying anything," I said. "Do you not want me to sponsor a child?"

The presenter had been so passionate about helping these children and teaching them about Jesus through the schools they set up that I was certain Oliver would want to help.

"I just don't understand why we would put money toward helping sponsor a child, when we could put money toward adopting one," Oliver said.

I was floored. I thought of all the prayers we had prayed together, asking God about adoption, waiting for the right moment. All those prayers had been met with a lack of peace and no confidence that God wanted us to move forward. I begged God to let us adopt, laying down all my demands, one by one, sacrificing them at God's feet just so I could hear a resounding yes in my spirit.

God, I want to adopt a baby from China, but if you need us to adopt an older girl, we will.

God, if we're not supposed to adopt from China, it's okay. I can still love China in other ways.

Oh, God, if you don't want us to adopt a girl, we'll adopt a boy. We can have five sons. God, we just want to honor you and take care of an orphan. We want to rescue a child and love him or her like you would. We'll obey any direction you give us. We just want to hear from you.

All that pleading, until finally, one day, I laid my whole heart bare in prayer.

God, if you don't want us to adopt a child, show us another way to help.

I looked at Oliver's face. His smile seemed charged with the same electricity that emanated from my heart. We felt certain God was saying, *Yes. Now. Go.*

❧❧❧

We both felt the complete upheaval of our lives in such a short period. Some days, I felt dizzy from the prospect of all the work ahead of us. After learning that adopting a healthy baby girl from China meant six years of waiting, we decided that we could take on limited special needs to cut the wait to just four years. We filled out mountains of paperwork and prepared our home for our home study. We talked to our boys about welcoming a new sister.

I tried to ignore the nudge in my heart that said we should adopt another child from China sometime in the future so that our daughter would have someone in our family who shared her culture. At that time, China would not adopt to parents who had more than four children in your home, so I tried to dismiss the thought of another child from China as some strange tangent of my brain and not an important direction to follow.

Just when I thought we had everything in order, I attended an adoption workshop from America World Adoption Association. They were not the agency we were using for our adoption, but I just needed a reminder that all this work was worth it. They said the wait for a girl with special needs was just one to two years. We didn't want to start the paperwork all over again or go through another home study, but having our daughter in our arms two years faster seemed like it would be worth all the trouble. So we started again.

భావ

"I'm honored to give Charlotte and her husband, Oliver, a chance to share a little bit with you about what God is doing in their family."

Pastor Nick handed me the microphone, and I looked out at our church family. My heart raced as I thought about what I wanted to say. If only words existed that could convince them that loving the people God loves is how we live like Jesus. I feared my words couldn't put my passion into their hearts.

Oh, God, do what only you can do. Stir up their hearts. Break their hearts for orphans the way you've broken ours.

"We are adopting a daughter from China. Of course, adoption is expensive, and we need to raise money, but we also wanted to think of a way that we could help orphans right now, while we raise money and wait to be matched with a little girl to bring home. We wanted you, our church family, to be able to do something for orphans, to care about them in a tangible way, while you help our family adopt. So we brought 100 blankets for orphans. We're calling them hope blankets. We would love for you to sponsor a hope blanket for $25. Take it home with you and pray over it. Pray for the orphan who will receive this blanket, and teach your kids to pray for the orphan who will be wrapped up in your family's hope blanket. Bring the blanket back here in six weeks, and we will send all the blankets to orphanages in China."

My husband held my arm and smiled at me, showing his silent, unwavering support.

One by one, the blankets disappeared, taken into

homes. *If only families opened their home to orphans as quickly as they opened their homes to these blankets,* I thought.

God, as these families pray over their hope blanket, show them that a very real child in need of love is waiting for this blanket and for a family. Change their hearts through these blankets, and honor all the prayers to bless 100 precious orphans. Thank you, Jesus.

ৰ্ৰ্ৰ্

Thank you, Jesus!

I had to stifle the desire to shout out my excitement. Family after family brought their hope blanket up to the front of the church. One hundred hope blankets, loved and prayed for, spread out in one place before God.

Everyone crowded around the blankets and prayed together that God would bless the orphans who would receive these blankets and give them families. Then they prayed for our family and for Gia, the daughter I already loved but whom I had not met. I had never heard her cry out for me, never held her in my arms, but I knew she was waiting somewhere in China for me, even though she didn't know I existed.

We took the blankets home that night, and I packed them up throughout the week. I dropped the blankets at the shipping center and drove home, where a giant rainbow spread across the sky just above my house for the second time. Crying, I took photo after photo, amazed to realize that this day was special not just to me, but to God, too.

❧❧❧

Joy filled my heart as I explained to my husband what the woman from America World Adoption Association told me that afternoon.

"They call it a special focus program. China just started it, but once we are matched with an orphan and the placement is accepted, we can adopt another orphan if we can be matched again in time. This means that we could bring home two orphans from China on the same trip."

"What?" I watched Oliver's face as he tried to process my words. The adoption process felt like the biggest adventure we ever took together. It felt like every day we had to make sense of some new obstacle or opportunity.

I tried to slow down, but my heart raced.

"If we can be matched with a second child within three weeks of them matching us with Gia, then we could adopt two orphans at once."

"I thought China limited how many children you could have in a family?"

"Not with this program. They don't place limitations, except that the second child has to be a child China considers a 'special focus,' which can mean they have multiple medical needs or more serious needs."

Oliver sat down and looked up at me. "Can we take

care of two children with special needs adjusting to a new home, new language and new culture, in addition to our four boys?"

"I don't know. It just felt like something I couldn't ignore, because I wanted to adopt a second child, but then I thought we couldn't have a second child from China. And now we can, and it feels like a miracle."

"We talked about adopting a second child after a few years. I don't know if we can do this. It would increase the costs for the adoption. We don't have a car for a family of eight. The needs of the second child would have to be something we could manage. It would take about a million miracles for this to happen."

"That's fine. God is a God of a million miracles. If he wants this to happen, it will."

"Okay. Let's take it one step at a time."

❧❧❧

One by one, each obstacle fell away, and we moved forward with the plan to adopt two children from China.

We learned that boys in China urgently needed homes. We hadn't realized how many boys in China were available to adopt, often because they have special needs. We mailed in our paperwork, and the wait began.

The week of Mother's Day, I received a wonderful gift in the form of an email.

"Oliver, come look at this," I said. "They sent us photos of the orphans with the hope blankets."

I stared at a beautiful baby snuggled up with a blanket we had shipped to China. One of the families in our church would see this photo and recognize the blanket they prayed over.

"Oh, wow," said Oliver. "I'm so glad they sent photos. What a cute baby!"

The next photo showed a child smiling brightly, with a hope blanket perched on his shoulder. I could not tell if the children in the photos were boys or girls.

"Look at these two, with the blankets on their heads," I said. "I just want to scoop them up."

Oliver reached over and pointed at the baby with the incredible smile. "I think that's the same baby from the first photo."

"Are you sure?" I carefully compared the first photo with the baby Oliver had pointed out.

"Yes, look. And that baby is in this photo, too. That baby loves to pose for photos."

I picked up another photo. "Here's the same baby again."

The baby, whom we began to refer to as "the hope blanket baby," appeared in six of the nine photos that we received.

We showed the photos at church on Mother's Day. The families at our church loved seeing the photos and realized that their very simple act of love had an impact on these precious children across the globe.

One woman from church asked me, "What if one of those babies in the pictures will be yours?" I tried not to laugh at the very sincere question, because I knew that China held close to a million orphans waiting for homes.

ॐॐॐ

I hated the waiting. I tracked our paperwork online so that I would know the exact day that it arrived in China. The paperwork arrived in China on September 12, but it was not processed and logged in to the system officially until September 13. I marveled. The date the baby we lost was due to be born, the date of a beautiful rainbow over our home and the date our paperwork officially entered the system in China.

ॐॐॐ

The waiting got more difficult. The weeks passed slowly. The woman helping us at America World Adoption Association told me that six other families were on the list ahead of us. We weren't going to be matched anytime soon.

In the middle of cooking a batch of treats, I felt my phone vibrate in my pocket. I ignored it while I finished up and then checked my voice mail.

"Hi, Charlotte. This is Karen. I have a referral for a baby girl I'd like you to look at. Why don't you give me a call back as soon as you can? We can talk about the match, and you can let me know if you want me to send you the file."

I couldn't call back fast enough. Karen told me a little about the baby. She was born prematurely and was very small. There was a slim possibility that she had been exposed to hepatitis B. I kept waiting for the complication, the scary medical news that might cause us to reevaluate, but none came. I asked her to send the file.

I sat at the computer and hit refresh repeatedly, waiting for the file to come. Finally, the email appeared in my inbox. I opened the file and clicked on the photos.

There she was. This baby must be my Gia. She was the tiniest thing I had ever seen. Her skinny little bird arms poked out from a pink onesie. I fell completely in love with her.

"You're mine, little girl," I said. "You are God's gift to me. I can't wait to bring you home."

Oliver was at karate across town with the boys. I called him, anyway. I couldn't wait.

His cellphone rang in the bedroom.

Of all the days to leave his phone here. I could have just strangled him. He had to see her!

I tried to be patient. I sat back at the computer and read the file. I checked the time. I couldn't wait for karate practice to end. I looked up the number for the dojo online. I called, and our friend who owned the dojo answered the phone.

"Hi, this is Charlotte. It's not an emergency — everything is fine — but could you have Oliver call me right away?"

"I'll get him for you."

"Thanks."

When Oliver came to the phone, he sounded worried. "Charlotte, what's wrong?"

"Nothing. Nothing's wrong at all. We have a referral, and she's so beautiful!"

"Now, don't get too attached," Oliver said. "We have to run everything by a doctor."

"It's too late. I love her. I really think she's our Gia. Come home and see her."

When Oliver arrived home, I showed him the photos from the file. I watched his face as he saw hers. I knew this little girl would steal his heart.

"So?"

"We just have to wait," he said. "The information in the file is three months old. We need to get her updated information, and the agency won't let us request the update until we've had a doctor review this file."

He's always so careful and practical, I thought. *It's probably good that I have him to balance me out.*

Our doctor said that the file looked good, and we requested the updated information. I showed everyone Gia's photo on our phone. Oliver waited. He didn't even call her Gia, let alone show her photo to his friends.

We received the updated file, which showed us how well she was growing. The file contained a photo of Gia sitting up on her own and smiling.

Suddenly, Oliver couldn't wait to show everyone this new photo of our daughter.

With an official match, we had just three weeks to find

a match for a second baby. Until this phase of the process, we'd barely tolerated how slowly the adoption process moved, but suddenly it was moving too quickly for us. We waited for referrals for a second baby, but none came. I began to search online, looking frantically to find a second child to bring home. All my searching only served to stress me out. It brought us no closer to a second child to bring home from China. I finally decided to trust God.

You put the idea of a second child in my heart, I told him. *You will have to make this happen, because all of my best efforts are failing.*

I started to lose hope that we would be able to adopt a second baby. However, I couldn't get one baby from the adoption website out of my heart. His needs were well beyond what we agreed to take on. He was malnourished, and he had the possibility of mental delays and a medical condition that I couldn't even pronounce. Still, something about him captivated me.

I called Karen and told her I wanted to know more about the boy on the website.

"You're not approved for his needs," she said.

"I know, but I think we might be willing to take on a little more."

"I will have to get special approval for you to even look at his file."

She called back a few hours later, letting me know that they had approved us for his needs. She emailed the file.

I wanted to click on the photos, but I knew I needed to know more about him. The photos would win me over, so

I forced myself to wait until I understood his circumstances.

Most files listed straightforward facts. This boy's file described how bright he was and how well he was doing. His medical condition was a blood issue. It could be as minor as low blood platelets or as serious as leukemia. I waited to look at his photos until a doctor could tell us more.

The doctor got back to us quickly. "Everything in his file looks really good. As far as I can tell, he has a very mild case of low blood platelets. It is likely something he would grow out of entirely, but if not, it would mean a daily medication."

Medicine every day. That's it? That was the only thing keeping me from saying yes to this sweet little face?

Oliver agreed that his needs were something we could take on. We finally opened the photos.

"Look at that face! He is a charmer."

Just like I had fallen in love with Gia at a single glance, I already felt like this playful boy was mine. His eyes shone with life and spunk.

"He's so funny, the way he poses for the camera," I said. "Oh, I love him."

Photo after photo showed him full of joy. As I looked over the photos, I stopped.

"Look, is that …"

"Oh, wow, I think you're right."

Oliver looked as shocked as I felt.

"It's the hope blanket baby."

"This is the hope blanket baby." Oliver's words hung in the air.

It seemed impossible. Almost a million babies were waiting for a family in China. I opened up the photos we received of orphans with the hope blankets, and there was no question. Our son was the hope blanket baby who'd won our hearts already.

We spent our evenings reading the files and noticed something amazing. Most babies had estimated birthdays. But when our son's biological parents abandoned him at the orphanage, they left a note that only contained a single piece of information — his birthday was February 12.

He shared a birthday with our youngest son, Joseph. It seemed that God was redeeming the loss of our first child with not one, but two babies.

A million little miracles later, we had two children waiting for us to come and pick them up in China.

చాచాచా

Snuggled up in our arms, our new son, Locke, and daughter, Gia, slept. The long flight home gave Oliver and me a chance to process it all.

My heart finally felt full. After months of feeling as if a part of me was lost across the ocean, I relished feeling their little hearts pressed against ours.

I looked at Oliver. He was starting to doze off. I knew I should let him sleep if he could, but I reached for his hand.

"You finally came to China with me."

"It is just as beautiful as you described," he said.

"I can't wait to have our whole family together in one place for the first time."

"Just a few more hours now, Charlotte."

"I'm so tired. I just want to cry and cry and never stop."

"I know what you mean. I can't believe we really did this. All the work was worth it, and just as soon as we get home, we can start building a life for our new, bigger family." As he spoke, his eyes shone with tears.

❧❧❧

I walked past cribs, struggling to believe that I was really back in China again. I was in Gia's orphanage in Q City, on a volunteer trip. This time, I brought friends from a Bible study I taught along with me. We joined other volunteers from around the world to update files on babies waiting for adoption. We loved each of these babies, holding them and playing with them. Some of the children with severe special needs were rarely touched or held in the orphanage, but they came to life with a little love.

If anyone had asked me the year before if there were any way I would take another trip to China, I would have said no. Our six children at home completely sapped all my energy and destroyed all my ideas of tidiness and organization. Happy chaos filled our lives, and most days I didn't know if the children had gone to school with matching socks or if anyone had combed his or her hair.

We were all overwhelmed, but I watched my four older boys fall in love with their new brother and sister. God had taken a family that had lost a baby, and two babies who had lost their families, and put them together. He knit us together as one big family growing every day in joy and compassion. It didn't matter anymore if life felt perfect — it was full of love.

I walked past a crib and stopped. A child sat with his head bowed down, so still, so quiet. I ran my hand over his head, and he tilted his face up toward mine. He smiled broadly, completely transforming his face with joy. I picked him up and held him. With each moment that passed, my heart belonged to him a little more fully.

He was blind. That little crib contained his whole world, and I needed to know that he would get to feel the sun on his face, hear the sounds of leaves rustling in the wind and feel the warm skin of a mother's face pressed against his.

I asked God for a name, and one immediately popped into my mind. Jeremy. I wanted Jeremy, but I knew I couldn't be his mom. My life already felt like more than I could manage. But I couldn't leave him in his dark cage, alone. When we left, would anyone rock him and sing to him? Would he receive tickles and kisses and hugs? Jeremy deserved to be loved. Would anyone love him?

When our group left, my heart broke. I found out that Jeremy had once been eligible for adoption, and I asked if they would reinstate his papers if I could find a family for him. They agreed. Through tears, I vowed to myself that I would find Jeremy's mom. The flight home nearly destroyed me. I knew my heart should leap at the thought of rejoining my six children, but I could only think of the child I left in Q City, China.

God, why this child? Why break my heart for a child I can't have? Help me find his mommy.

I wrote Jeremy's story and shared it everywhere I could. Later, I looked up the name Jeremy. It meant "appointed by God."

Someone has to love Jeremy like I do. Someone has to want to be his mommy. He is the appointed one. God saw him in his darkness, like a hidden treasure. Someone else will understand how precious he is.

Someone did. She read his story and contacted me. She is raising money now, waiting, as I struggled to wait, for the day when she can finally bring Jeremy home and spend a lifetime teaching him that he is loved. Not just by his new American family, but also by the God of a million little miracles.

CONCLUSION

"I will meditate on all your work and muse on all your
deeds. Your way, O God, is holy; what God is great like
our God? You are the God who works wonders;
You have made known your strength among the peoples."
(Psalm 77:12-14 KJV)

After reading these stories, I am more convinced than
ever that God is the God who works wonders, who moves
mountains on behalf of orphans and the vulnerable, who
is "the Father to the Fatherless" and the one who "delights
to set the lonely in families."

In Isaiah 45:3, we find this promise: "I will give you
treasures hidden in the darkness — secret riches ... so that
you may know that I am the Lord."

That's what he did for me. And for each of us who
journeyed together to Q City.

We found these treasures in the cradles. Precious little
boys and girls — treasures in the darkness, unknown and
unseen by the world.

We found God there among them. I've never been
more certain that he knows each precious child by name,
knows the number of hairs on each head, created each one
and declared them "fearfully and wonderfully made." We
experienced God's presence in powerful and amazing
ways. Our time in Q City was holy and unforgettable.

We did not come home the same.

We could not erase those faces, those smiles, those tears from our hearts. We were broken for them. After we met the orphans in Q City, we realized that, suddenly, all orphans had become real and personal. Each had a face. Each had a name.

By some estimates, 147 million orphans worldwide do not have enough food. Do not have enough love. Have no one to sing to them, to hold them, to tell them that they are not forgotten. Have no chance for education and no hope for the future.

And we are not okay with that.

God had broken our hearts for the things that break his heart. So we took our broken hearts to him. We cried out for these treasures, asking God to move, asking God to make a way for them, asking God to show us what he would have us do.

We laid our lives at his feet, and we put our "yes" on the table to whatever way God would choose to use us to care for the least of these.

And what he has done through each feeble, fearful "yes" is nothing short of miraculous.

Nine of our team members said yes to adoption.

Six of our team members now volunteer with Love Without Boundaries.

Three team members are training to become foster parents.

Two team members are now leading mission teams of their own.

Four children who had either been waiting years to be adopted or were never even registered for adoption are now coming home.

Fifteen children have received life-saving medical care and surgeries through Love Without Boundaries.

A Love Without Boundaries Believe in Me School has been started right in the orphanage for children who did not qualify for public education because of medical or developmental needs.

Nutrition is improving.

Dental care is now being emphasized.

Babies are being held, touched and sung to because the nannies now understand how vital this is for growth and development.

Relationships and trust are being built with the orphanage staff.

The orphanage, once somber and oppressive, now has a spirit of life and hope.

Best of all, the light and love of Jesus is shining brightly in this place, across language and cultural barriers, and eternities are being changed.

So what does this have to do with you? Everything, if you, too, have a heart for the poor, forgotten and brokenhearted.

As a Christ follower, I could not ignore that Christ came to bring good news to the poor, to bring comfort to the brokenhearted and freedom to those in darkness. Over and over in his word, he tells us to bring justice to the vulnerable. To care for those in need. He tells us to love because we have been loved. To rescue because we have been rescued. To give because he has given so much for us.

And so, how can I not?

James 2:15-16 reads, "Suppose a brother or sister is without clothes and daily food. If one of you says to him, 'Go, I wish you well; keep warm and well fed,' but does nothing about his physical needs, what good is it? In the same way, faith without works is dead."

God's word became clearer to me on that trip to Q City. His heart is for the orphan, the widow, the poor. I realized that, if I am his, then I will have this heart as well, and it will be reflected in my life being poured out for the voiceless, the powerless.

"Pure and genuine religion in the sight of God the Father means caring for orphans and widows in their distress and refusing to let the world corrupt you" (James 1:27).

Timothy Keller, an American pastor and theologian, says this: "Many who are evidently genuine Christians do not demonstrate much concern for the poor. How do we account for that? I would like to believe that a heart for the poor 'sleeps' down in the Christian's soul until it is awakened."

It is my hope that God uses the hidden treasures in the cradles in Q City to awaken more and more hearts. May he give each of us a passion for his precious ones and compel us to go and be his hands and feet to the least of these.

CONCLUSION

"And the King will reply, 'I tell you the truth, whatever you did for one of the least of these brothers of mine, you did for me'" (Matthew 25:40).

Ashley Gosnell
Storyteller Missions Team Member
October 2014 & October 2015

Ways to Make a Difference

- Pray
- Donate to America World Adoption or to Love Without Boundaries (LWB)
- Follow Facebook pages for America World Adoption, Storyteller Missions and LWB
- Help with medical expenses for orphans through LWB
- Go on a trip
- Adopt a child
- Help a single mom
- Connect with a local church in your area, and get involved in their initiatives
- Give money, prayers and practical support to adopting families
- Show kindness to someone with a physical disability
- Show kindness to the abandoned, homeless, hungry, immigrant and imprisoned
- Pray some more

To learn more about how YOU can get involved in orphan care, or to find resources and answers to commonly asked questions, please visit www.cradlesinqcity.wordpress.com or email CradlesInQCity@gmail.com.